Swimming the River

Susan Carter Payne

Raven Wylie Press

Virginia Beach, Virginia

Swimming the River is the second part of the **Responsible Living** series and continues the journey of **Stepping into the Wilderness.** This volume continues the exploration of relationship and discovery of self.

There are many facets of self and relationship. Learning to express ourselves through creative outlets gives each of us a voice. The passions that drive our creativity and daily lives also enable us to define our purpose. It takes courage and trust to assess ourselves and relationships. By loving ourselves regardless of our mistakes but still holding ourselves accountable to our own thoughts, actions, and reactions we can establish honest and deep connections with others. We are on this journey of life together and each benefit from one another's support.

Responsible Living

Starts with Self

Develops Trust

Requires Courage

Promotes Forgiveness

Removes Guilt

Focuses on Love

Abides by Peace

Endures by Faith

Continues through Hope

Results in Happiness

PART ONE

DESIRE, DREAMS, AND CREATIVITY

We are driven by desire and purpose.
These are the wings from which our
dreams are born. When we take flight we
begin to express from the heart, the
creator of art.

Coming into Your Own

There is no better person to be than you. Only you can fulfill your purpose.

You are here at this place and time for a reason. Whether or not you understand the circumstances or the timing, know you belong where you are at this moment.

Every day you become a little bit more of whom you are going to become. Give yourself room to grow. Look for the lessons in your mistakes.

Don't reconcile to be one of the others; be the person you were born to be. Know that you were made in the image of love.

Remember you hold the power to be anything you want. Feel good about the person you are; you are one of a kind. Know you are special.

Take your dreams into reality; don't settle for less than you deserve. Let your inner wisdom be your compass. Let commitment and faith be your pavers. Be accountable to yourself today because it will make a difference tomorrow. Every step upon the path is one closer to where you are going.

Recognize the yearnings of your heart; listen as they whisper to you. Awaken to the music of your soul; stand up and dance.

Love what makes you uniquely you. Make the choice to be happy every day. Live with an attitude of gratitude.

Care not what others think; free yourself. Trust to live as the beautiful soul you are.

Don't fear life's lessons; live life from the inside out. Have the courage to be where you are and go where you need to go.

Be aware of your blessings each step of the journey. Allow yourself to feel the joy along the way. Know you are capable.

If you can dream it, you can believe it.

If you can believe it, you can breathe it.

If you can breathe it, you can achieve it.

When you achieve it, you will live it.

Wading in the Creek:

In what ways do you feel you are a product of your parents/family?

How do you stand out in a group of people?

Have you ever accomplished something others said you weren't capable of?

When have you settled by doing what someone else wanted you to do rather than what you wanted?

Why are you afraid or empowered to follow your dreams?

Swimming the River:

Write a story about a face of courage.

Write a personal narrative/memoir about a failure never admitted.

Write a poem about authenticity.

Write a scene about someone breathing life into a dream.

Write a dialogue between an overconfident person and a capable yet unsure person.

House of Sacredness

Remember you were created with a consecrated mission.

You are a house of sacredness. You were created with love and bathed in light.

Your light shines. The Light shines on you. You are the light.

Holiness resides within you. You are a blessing to the world. You are loved. Love in return.

Your very breath is holy. Life is a miracle. You are consecrated. Exalt those you touch and those who touch you.

When the wind blows through the trees, do not be shaken. Fear not, for courage is within you. Know the Light also shines through those very same trees.

Trust beyond yourself. Have faith your needs will be met.

Know the Light will lead you through the darkness.

Know the path of life will be lit for you.
Know the Light will guide you home.
Let your light shine, and follow where it takes you.
Shine on.

Wading in the Creek:
How do you keep your light shining?
Do you feel your light is strong enough to lead you
through dark times?
In what ways do you light a path for others?
Do you follow the light of your own path?
What assures you this light will guide you?

Swimming the River:
Write an emotional personal narrative/memoir about
floundering in the darkness.
Write a scene showing someone exhibiting emotional
or physical courage.
Write a Lyric poem based on your thoughts of
darkness and light.
Describe a portion of your life's path as the setting for
a short story.
Write a descriptive piece about the entrance of light
(person or thing) into your life.

Traveling Through the Desert

Never be afraid to tap into the stream of creativity which flows within you.

Being an East Coast girl I've vacillated between mountains and sea. The desert has always been a mystery to me. When I finally experienced my first taste of the desert, I found the magnitude of the mountains intimidating as I hiked my way through them. Still, I felt the warmth of the same sun upon my back in the day and lay my head beneath the same moon at night.

I expected the desert to be lifeless with the exception of scorpions, snakes, tarantula, and thorny cacti. In other words, I considered desert life forms to be dangerous. What a delight awaited my senses. We did not encounter a single snake or scorpion. We only came upon three tarantulas who were not bothered by us in the least.

What a surprise it was to view the flow of subtle green across the landscape. The combination of brush sage, juniper, cacti, and desert flowers cast a usual and continuous fragrance throughout the mountains and barren lands. The aroma was both floral and spicy, yet smelled of musky earth. Tree roots stretched across the sand, clinging to rocks, grasping for a chance to reach for the sun. If we can adopt this same degree of tenacity we can create in times of emptiness.

Often life feels like we are traveling through the desert. We become parched. We complain there is no stream to quench our thirst. Our creativity wanes, and we think we've become a barren wasteland. Life is abundant in those so called wastelands. There is always enough water for desert life to thrive, and such it is with us. We forget to tap into our own resources. We store everything we need inside. It is our own doubt and fears that keep us from moving in the direction we dream. When things get thorny we'd soon blame the cacti rather than take responsibility. Thorns are simply the defense mechanism of the cacti while we have our own defense mechanisms such as denial and avoidance. When we become familiar with ourselves, knowing our own needs and knowing how to provide these for ourselves rather than depending on others, we can thrive like the desert sage.

There are times in the desert that one must simply learn to adapt in order to survive. We must root ourselves in confidence to sustain the harsh dusty winds. If we trust in our abilities, we will never become tumbleweeds among the desert floor.

Art births from vision. We can imagine what we want to create. We can move to the music of our muse. We can become the flowering cacti on the canvas of desert sand.

Wading in the Creek:

Have you ever found your perception of something to be totally different than your own expectations?
Have you found it to be true as well as people you've gotten to know?
In what ways are you not watering the vegetation of your own dreamland?
Have you allowed yourself to become a wasteland?
What steps can you take to flourish?

Swimming the River:

Write about a friendship (you or someone you know) that started out as a relationship of distrust or animosity.
Write about a food you hated as a kid but now love.
Write in your child's voice, and then again in your adult perspective.
Write a story about someone who thinks he/she needs a talisman to accomplish something important and finds he has the ability within himself.
Write a Cinquain poem about the desert.
Make a list of all your resources related to your talent/dream. Write a letter of encouragement to yourself stating the argument of how you have exactly what you need to take the next step toward your dream.

Getting Your Feet Wet

Walk until you're ready to run, and when you're ready don't let anything stand between you and the finish line.

Does your true desire call your name?
Does the sound of the roar frighten you?
Step off the bank. Wade in. Get your feet wet.
Even if you can't see the bottom, you must trust.
Let the water flow over you. Let it wash the fear away.
Practice your art. Live your life. Be the best at who you are.

Float until you learn to swim. Go with the ebb and flow.
Ride the wave. Become the wave. Be your passion.
Write words until sentences form. Turn sentences into paragraphs and paragraphs into chapters. Tell your story, and the book will arrive.
Stroke by stroke, paint the canvas with color and texture. Allow the image of your heart to appear.
Play with subject, light and shadow. Aim and shoot until the perfect photograph emerges.
Smooth the cold ragged edges of stone. Chisel the rock until the shape that calls you is formed.
Let your fingers do the dance of life. Play the chords until the song sweeps your soul away.
What do you dream of? What haunts you? Let the rhythm of your spirit guide you. Show the world what moves you and you will move the world.

Wading in the Creek:
In what parts of your life do you give your best at all times?
What feeds your soul in your current line of work?
How do the people in your life support your spirit?
In what ways does your courage encourage you to take risks with your talents?
How does your view of your abilities conflict or agree with how others perceive them?
Give your muse a name, and write a story about a visit with your muse.

Swimming the River:
Write about when you came to realize your talent.
Does this skill come naturally or do you work to perfect it?
Write a personal narrative/memoir about encouraging a talent.

Write a name or acrostic poem about your talent. Write a personal essay about being energized or depleted from indulging in your gift. Include how you maintain balance during the creative process or in times of creative drought.

Take Me to the Woods

Nothing ignites the passion of the soul quite like nature.

Take me to the woods.
I want to fill my lungs of the earth.
I want to breathe in the dampness of the early morning air.
I want to watch the sun rise over the tree tops.
I want to taste the morning mist as it settles into the moss and fern.
I want to envelope the scent as the pine and cedar mingle.

I want to push my way through the thickets.
I want to feel the tickle of the wind against my neck.
I want to hear the drum of the woodpecker as it echoes through the forest.
I want to search for the fine line where earth blends to sky.
I want to shuffle through the leaves and forge my own path.
I want to settle my soul into this world of mine.
Take me to the woods...

Wading in the Creek:
How does nature speak to you?
Are you senses aroused when among the elements?
Do you lose track of time when there are no distractions?
In what ways do you feel a connection to something much greater than yourself?
When do you make time to just be in the midst of nature?

Swimming the River:
Write a story starting with "I knew I was lost when..."
Write a haiku about your favorite aspect of nature.
Write a personal narrative/memoir about spirit merging with any of the elements.
Write a scene set in the woods. Does the setting inspire or incite fear?
Write a short story with one of the elements as the voice.

Write like the Wind

Live like the wind by setting your own direction and pace.

I stand amongst the changing hues of avocado, crimson, pumpkin, and mustard. I watch the colors mingle as they tango across tree branches and stretch into an azure sky. The image changes with the breeze and the appearance of two bright white clouds rise above the distant mountain. Sun dapples fragments of soapstone strewn along the ocher road. Wind rattles off a song through the woods while my feet shuffle another melody through the fallen leaves.

As I feel the gust whip beneath my sweater, I watch the limbs bend a path. I wonder where I'll end up if I choose to follow. I question if I have what it takes to bend a path rather than following one.

I stop and close my eyes. I smile at the thought of the wind's wildness, its reckless abandon…the pure freedom to travel its choice of speed and direction. I envy its power, but only for a moment. Oh, how I've wanted my writing to be as free and wild as the wind… I realize I do have that same power. Yes, I do. I think about the ability to move as quickly or slowly as desired without expectations or demands. I understand I am the one who places pressure upon me.

I choose to write like the wind. I will set the pace and follow my heart. I refuse to feel guilty about my writing choices. I will not criticize my every word. I will write like the wind.

The leaves lift into the air and shimmer in the sunlight. And for a moment, I am the wind. Swoosh! Step into your art and let the wind be your guide…swoosh!

Wading in the Creek:

Have you chosen to bend your own path or to follow one before you?

What is the one thing that calls you above all others? What are your long term objectives?

How have you built confidence to pursue your dream? In the midst of your plans, how do you manage to enjoy life in the moment?

Swimming the River:

Write a personal narrative/memoir about drawing inspiration the environment.

Write a poem about the forming of a path.

Write a story centering on a lack of freedom.
Write a scene of two people in the heat of a competition.
Write a short story using wind as your main character. What time is the action taking place? Use your setting to advance the wind's intention.

On Being the Little Red Caboose

Be sure to live like the champion of your story.

We all long to be the hero/heroine of our story. The problem is that we forget we are also the author.
Most of us want to be respected and admired, or at least valued and accepted for who we are.
We yearn for our true worth to shine, yet we often struggle with production.
We seldom give it all we've got because we're afraid we won't shine as brightly as others in our field.

Or worse, we're afraid we'll have to stand alone.
When we're not crowded we have room to grow.
Sometimes those of us who stand alone shine the brightest of all.
While it's true we don't have complete control of all life circumstances and our resources might be limited, we do have the power to make choices. Even the caboose can be the conductor of his train.
You might feel like you're pushing your way through life in a constant uphill battle. Use that strength and stamina to the best of your ability.
We might not be the little red caboose that saves the train from rolling down the mountain, but we each can be the little red caboose of our own story. Be the hero in your life.
Recognize your talents. Trust yourself to use them. Hone your gifts.
You are powerful.
You are awesome.
Push that train over the mountain!
Shine, baby, shine!

Wading in the Creek:
Do you see yourself as the hero/heroine of your story?
Do you know how to use your talents to benefit your life?
Do you believe in yourself as much as others believe in you?
What steps can you take to build confidence in your gifts?
What is preventing you from trusting yourself?

Swimming the River:
Write a personal narrative about an uphill battle.

Write "The Little Red Caboose" as your story. Who or what is your steam engine? Who or will you save and how?

Write a story about someone discovering a supernatural power.

Write a poem titled Awesome.

Write a dialogue between a band or music teacher and a student. Have the teacher convince the student to do a solo. What might the teacher say to instill confidence in the student?

Living Life the Best We Can

When all is said and done we will find times of imbalance are what shaped and strengthened us to become who we are.

There are times in life that we feel like everyone wants a piece of us. They seem to grab us and hang on for the ride. They literally suck the life out of us. We feel stifled, smothered, and tangled. We all must learn to say "no".

Other times, we worry until we tend to manifest knots throughout our bodies and souls. We think everyone's well-being is up to us. We feel we can't let the people we love down. We must gather the strength to make necessary changes because a good massage just isn't enough to take care of us.

We get hit at from every angle until we are filled with holes. We don't have enough of a foundation to hold ourselves together. When we take care of our own needs we are more capable to nurture those around us.

We can become twisted and bent, and seem to be reaching in all the wrong directions. We seem to have lost our balance in life. We've forgotten what is important. We've thrown away our dreams for the sake of others or maybe we're depressed and cease to dream at all. While it's good to be flexible, sometimes we do need to refocus and prioritize the people and things in our lives. We are better off to slow down and take one moment at a time.

We can't all be the big sprawling Oak tree that stretches, endures, and flourishes while letting nothing hinder its growth. The Oak started as an acorn with big dreams, and so can we. Regardless, we still need to reach for the sky.

The sun doesn't always warm our shoulders. At times, bitter winds bite at our faces. Some days our paths are less clear than others. We just need to keep walking with our eyes on the Light above and trust that it will guide us home.

Wading in the Creek:

How have you practiced saying "no"?

What steps do you take to ensure worry does not rule your life?

How has reaching for dreams had a negative effect on your life?

When has trust kept you afloat during a tough time?

What dreams have you managed to achieve?

Swimming the River:

Write about a time you said "no" when you were pressured to say "yes".

Write a poem about floating on a dream.

Write a scene set in a tree house built in a sprawling Oak. Describe the climb up and what might view from there.

Write a story in which someone is guided by a light.

Write a dialogue of someone trying to convince someone else to say yes. Make convincing arguments for both sides.

Within the Flow

The best way to travel is in the flow.

At times we drift along, unaware of where we've been or where we're going. We sort of just go along for the ride. We can sink, or become stagnant, and we often hang on for the sake of it with no intentions in mind. There are situations where we need to absorb our surroundings before we can move on. Significant events can happen in our lives or in the lives of those we love and we must tread water to stay afloat until we are able to swim again.

We tend to get so comfortable in life variations upset our confidence. We don't welcome challenges and are not agreeable to change life sometimes dictates. We must filter our way through the best course putting in action all life lessons from our past.

Life flows like a mighty river. We're not always aware of every rock or waterfall and their purpose within our flow. We possibly know what we want, where we're headed, and even we think we know exactly how to get there, but one rock or limb of debris can alter our course. We must let nature take over and trust all will be well in the end.

We each approach the same vast deep ocean. Some fight against the flow. Some float while others tread water. The more experienced swim with the current. Eventually we learn to relax and accept the situation. Sometimes, faith and hope are all we have, and that's usually enough to keep our heads above water.

Wading in the Creek:
What keeps you afloat when you feel like you're sinking?
Do you find comfort in daily routine?
How do you deal with significant change?
Do you rebel against the majority?
Are you a pace setter?

Swimming the River:
Write a story about a canoe trip gone wrong.
Write a scene with fishermen fighting a river current.
Remember your setting can play a significant role in the outcome of your scene.
Write a poem about treading water.

Detail a setting containing debris. Include how it effects the environment and the people in the vicinity. Write a personal narrative/memoir about learning to swim.

Let Your Love Light Shine

When we are accountable to love, no fingers point blame.

Throughout our lives we deal with powerful emotions such as anger, blame, guilt, and fear. There are times, often through tragedy, that we experience all these emotions at once. It's a conflicting whirlpool that has the ability to drown us if we allow it.

Regret, guilt, and blame have no place in a heart who wants to move forward. Healthy relationships are based on love and acceptance. It all starts with self-responsibility. When we become responsible to ourselves we become respectful to ourselves and others. We alone are responsible for our own realities. Blame fills our lives with anxiety and stifles our personal growth, not to mention the guilt and devastation it places on others. I once had a pastor who said that whenever we point a finger at someone we have three more pointing back at us. Those words had a profound effect on me. I'm not saying I've never done it since, but usually in reflection I catch it and try to right my wrong. Blame should not be a way of life. The way to a fulfilling life is through self-responsibility, love, acceptance, and forgiveness.

Blame only succeeds in making others feel guilty which does nothing to solve the problem. The root is usually unhappiness for one reason or another of the person inflicting blame. Often people are afraid to explore why they feel the way they do. It takes a strong person with good values to reflect and mend. Finding fault does not create remedies. Accusations only cause more pain. Blame is simply a copout. We can't change circumstances or other people, but we can change ourselves and our perceptions. In fact, perceptions are another reason we blame others. We too often only see how things affect us. If we remove ourselves from the situation, things look much differently. Not everything in life is about us, and sometimes none of it is about us.

Self-responsibility starts with you and me. We might grow up with certain attitudes and tendencies but if we are wrong it is our own responsibility to fix ourselves. We need to make ourselves accountable. We may not be able to control all, but we each have the power to shape our own destiny. We have an obligation and an opportunity to do what is right. Acceptance and forgiveness are practices we should incorporate into our daily lives. We all have the ability to give and receive love. And truly at the end of the day, isn't that all we really want? When we take responsibility we are humbled and others place their trust in us, and we do the same in return. When we do this, our relationships flourish, and we as individuals expand. We touch others with our love and our lives, and they in turn do the same. We become ripples in the pond.

We waste too much time wallowing in the dark cave of self-pity when we can be out creating sunshine. When we've done right, we have peace in our hearts. That alone gives us the power to let the situation go and move on. Forgiveness releases us as much as the person we are forgiving. Forgiveness is freeing, like the sun rising each morning. May we each go out and be the sun in someone else's life.

Wading in the Creek:
When something goes wrong do you look for someone to blame?
Do you feel guilty when things work out for you but not for someone else?
Why do you or do you not accept responsibility for your actions?
Do your opinions cloud your judgment?
Do you look for the good in every person you meet?

Swimming the River:
Write a scene where two people accuse one another for something while a third person (the guilty party) stands by and watches the drama unfold.
Write a (Dramatic monologue) poem about destiny.
Write a personal narrative/memoir about taking a huge risk to do what is right.
Write a story portraying the ripple effect.
Set your scene in a dark cave. Have a small crack of sunlight streaming in. Tell what it looks like and how it makes the inhabitants feel. What do they do when they see this?

Dare to Dream

When you hear your passion raging above your own heartbeat, you owe it to yourself and to the world to stop humming and start singing.

We spend our whole lies waiting to be ripe.
We can't want to share our talents, but they never seem ready to harvest.
We feel seasoned, but we don't think other's see our full quality.
Sometimes we feel like an ordinary cornstalk in a corn field, all biding our time.
There are times we feel alone.
We think we're the single stalk standing while all have received their just rewards.
We wonder when our time will come.
Sometimes we must learn the virtue of patience and the benefit of solitude.
We fail to see we are eating away at ourselves.
We blame others rather than doing our own part.
Connecting helps us grow and reach our potential.

Sometimes we must hold tight to our dreams without eating the life from them.

Wading in the Creek:
Are you waiting for your time to come or has it come?
Do you feel like a loner or part of a group?
When have you had to be patient?
How do you benefit from solitude?
Do you feel like you are wasting away?

Swimming the River:
Write a short story with the setting a cornfield.
Write a poem about potential.
Write a personal narrative/memoir about being ordinary.
Write a dialogue between a cornstalk and a feeding crow.
Write a scene showing a network of people helping someone share his/her talent.

Swimming the Waters as We Build Upon the Shore

When we are moved enough to do it on our own, others are motivated to follow.

Whether you step into the water or walk upon the sand depends on where you wish to go.
Often we need to weave in and out to accomplish our goals.
We jump into the water for inspiration, ride the waves for energy, and float the current while we dream.
We scribble our thoughts into the sand.

We dig, pile and shape, building dreams upon the shore, our process visible in the sand.
Every time we need empowerment, we head to the water.
We leave a trail of footprints to water's edge.
The tide wipes out or proves the endurance of all we've accomplished.
We need water to purify our souls and sand to show us where we've been.
Who will run along the shore to follow us?
Who will jump in the water with us and swim the course?

Wading in the Creek:
Do you have someone you can count on to always be by your side?
Is there someone who counts on you to be by her side?
Does water have a healing or inspirational effect on you?
Have your dreams ever been washed away?
What proves you've been here?

Swimming the River:
Write a scene of someone writing or drawing something in the sand.
Write a poem about endurance.
Write a dialogue between the tide and someone running along the shoreline.
Write a personal narrative/memoir about strength.
Write a story about "castles in the sand".

Open Doors

When you realize you are the only thing holding you back, you will see the door has been open all along.

The door is open.
What are you waiting for?
What are you afraid of?
Take a chance, step inside.
You can't spend your entire life on the outside looking in.
Life looks a lot different from the inside looking out.
You'll never know if you don't step over the threshold.

Opportunity waits on the other side.
This is the time of your life.
It is waiting for you to step in and claim it.
This is what you've been waiting for…
Go for it!

Wading in the Creek:

When's the last time you took a chance.
Does risk frighten or excite you?
Would you rather view things from the outside looking
in or the inside looking out?
What have you waited a long time for?
Do you feel like you are part of a circle or group of
people?

Swimming the River:

Write a scene about someone "just looking".
Write a poem "inside out".
Write a personal narrative/memoir about a chance
meeting.
Write a story about someone watching from a
distance the coming and goings of a business
building.
Write about an opportunity you think is not available
to you because you are an outsider.

Traveling Through This World

If you follow your heart you will never be lost.

Careful the road you tread,
be it the well-worn path,
the traveled paved road,
the bumpy graveled route,
or the one where you bend
the grass beneath your feet.
Marvel at the view along the way.
Feel the warmth of the sun upon your back.
Listen to the wind as it speaks to you.

Take in the scent of all that is offered and bask in the
aroma.
Don't leave anything out.
Taste life as it meets you head on.
What you learn on the journey
is just as important as what you find
when you reach your destination.
What you do when you get there is up to you.
Yesterday's road brought you here.
There will be another one tomorrow.
Today, when your feet touch the ground
feel the sensation travel through your body.
Know this moment in time is yours
and the path is of your choosing.
Life is what you make of it.
Keep walking. The world is waiting for you.

Wading in the Creek:
Are you a list maker?
Do you keep to a schedule?
Have you ever been called a free spirit?
Do you prefer to walk or ride?
Where are you most alert to activity around you?

Swimming the River:
Take a nature walk and vividly describe all your
senses encounter.
Write a story about a schedule that can't be kept.
Write personal narrative/memoir about taking a wrong
turn.
Write a scene of feet touching the ground.
Write a poem about the taste of life.

Life's River of Harmony

Simplicity is the first step on the road to harmony.

When our foundations are shaky, we teeter as the rivers of life flow around us. Maybe our foundations are leaning because we've manipulated and rebuilt ourselves into a structure unable to endure.

We refuse to dive in. Perhaps we are afraid to submerge ourselves.

We barely even get our feet wet. Maybe we haven't learned how to swim. Or maybe we can but aren't strong enough to survive the current.

Sometimes we don't want to get our feet wet at all. We stay completely above water at all costs.

We might feel the need to pile rocks to fortify our base before we take the plunge. A single pebble strategically positioned can make the difference between standing and faltering.

Sometimes things are aligned perfectly. It just may be the way it is, or it might take lots of time and energy getting there. When you reach that point, you will feel your strength.

We learn and grow from the lessons life and nature throws our way. Occasionally we just want to sit back and take comfort in all that we know and all that we are. We feel the love and energy of the people around us. These are the times we enjoy basking in the beauty of all that surrounds us. There is sacredness within us and about us. We feel complete. Welcome to peace.

Wading in the Creek:

Are you easily swayed?
Do you feel your integrity is unshakeable?
When have you been persuaded to change your mind?
Why do you think you have strong or weak viewpoints?
What is your most solid characteristic?

Swimming the River:

Write a story about an intense fear of water.
Write an inner dialogue of someone trying to make a stand on an issue.
Write a scene of a crumbling foundation (physical or metaphorical).
Write about a time you couldn't make up your mind.
Write a poem about alignment.

If You Can't Bloom, Transplant Yourself

Changes for a more productive life must begin with you.

Bloom where you are planted, and if you can't, transplant yourself. See this little guy here? Isn't he stunning? We bought him over twelve years ago. He arrived with a bud and bloomed that year, but never again until now. Two years ago I transplanted him to another bed. I walked out of the house the other day, and to my great surprise he was in full bloom. Some plants and people just take their own sweet time. And sometimes, it's all about the soil.

There are times people need to pick themselves up and transplant into other gardens or they just need to fertilize the soil around them. We are given so many opportunities to reinvent our lives. While we are young, we are given the opportunity with each school transfer or move. The opportunity arises again with college or the work force. Then there is marriage, change of employment, new neighborhoods or churches, and community organizations or other social clubs. These are not our only means to recreate our lives. We have the power to do it any time we want.

I was a late bloomer in life. However, as soon as I blossomed I became what I thought the soil around me required me to be. The remainder of my flowers was hidden in my soul. With each stage in life, I attached to the other flowers in my garden, and still refused to allow the rare flower within to bloom. It took me many years to realize that all I needed to do to bloom was change the soil around me. I didn't need to fully transplant. I weeded my garden and cultivated my soul. Now, my life is in full bloom. It might not appear that way to others, but I feel the blooms deep inside shooting towards the sun.

I actually had to step out of my flowerpot to experience my growth. I had to make myself uncomfortable and experience new things. Even though I appeared the same for so many years, I think I was gradually taking shape. It took a little weeding and raking of my soul, some courage (fertilizer), and some experience (mulch). One day, I simply embraced my life and unfolded my petals.

There is hope in whoever you are today to become whoever you will be tomorrow. I'm not saying we can just name anything or anyone in the world and become that thing or person. I am saying that we each have within us the power to follow our dreams. We hold our abilities and desires deep within us. It's a matter of reaching deep inside and coming face to face with ourselves…and then, anything is possible.

Wading in the Creek:
Why have you ever felt the need to transplant?
Have you ever changed career paths?
Do you still have the same friends you had ten years ago?
What do you do to cultivate inner growth in your life?
When have you felt stunted or wilted?

Swimming the River:
Write about your first day on a new job.
Write a comparison of yourself to a flower that most accurately fits you.
Write a poem about a dying flower.
Write a story about a gardener/farmer and his unique use of fertilizer.
Write anything containing "When I looked in the mirror I couldn't believe it was me".

Choices

You get nowhere if you don't move forward. Don't think about where you'll land if you fail; concentrate on where you're headed if you succeed.

We stand at the corner post.
Do we go left or right?
One way is possibly success.
The other possibly failure...
But who is really to say?
Lessons don't always constitute success or failure;
It's simply knowledge gained.

So we climb atop the fence.
We see the grass is greener on the other side.
But have we measured the worth of the stones
among the grasses, flowers, and trees on our side?
Choices.
Do we jump off and run back where we came from?
Do we charge forth into the wilderness?
Besides, who said it's a point of no return?
One thing's for sure;
Sitting on the fence will get us anywhere.

Wading in the Creek:

Have you ever chosen the way you were discouraged
from taking?
Have you ever tried to talk others out of doing what
they felt they needed to do?
Would you prefer to sit on the fence post rather than
try something new?
Do you always feel like someone else's life is better
than your own?
In what ways do you own your choices?

Swimming the River:

Write a short story starting with "When the time
came…"
Write a poem about a heavy load.
Write a narrative about being encouraged to
undertake a new adventure.
Draw a character sketch of someone who is "sitting
on the fence".
Write a scene of someone walking into the unknown.

Fortifying Our Lives

**The walls we build to keep our hearts safe
are the same ones that keep us from being
happy.**

We build our walls with heavy stones.
We hope to hold the storms at bay.
We protect ourselves with jetties, laying one stone at
a time.
We pile indifference, anger, prejudice, resentment,
and fear
until our harbor can't be penetrated. Love and
kindness can't find their way to us...

and we blame others for our suffering.
When we don't make an effort to reach out, others
may grow tired of trying to tear down our barricades.
We are much less fragile than we think.
We don't realize enduring the storms make us
stronger.
Often the very things we fear don't pose a threat to
us.
We must be careful when we hide behind the wall; we
might possibly drown in a storm of our own making.
We don't need walls to fortify our lives. If we move
just one of those rocks,
we'll make a space for life-sustaining changes.
When we remove fear, we will allow love to enter.
Always, love leads the way…

Wading in the Creek:
When have you sought comfort behind walls?
What stones have you piled around you?
How did you remove those stones from your life?
How was your life enriched when you removed those
stones?
Have you ever been the light that penetrated
someone else's walls?

Swimming the River:
Write anything starting with "I never knew it could hurt
so much…"
Write a personal narrative of "Why I can't trust
him/her".
Write a poem depicting yourself as a stone structure
(examples -pile of stone, stone hedge, cairn, statue,
pyramid, sidewalk).
Write about a time in your life someone "loved you
through a rough time".

Write a story about a hermit being pestered by townspeople.

Unlocking the Heart

It is generally not the world who doesn't accept us as we are. We are the ones who dare ourselves to truly be as we are.

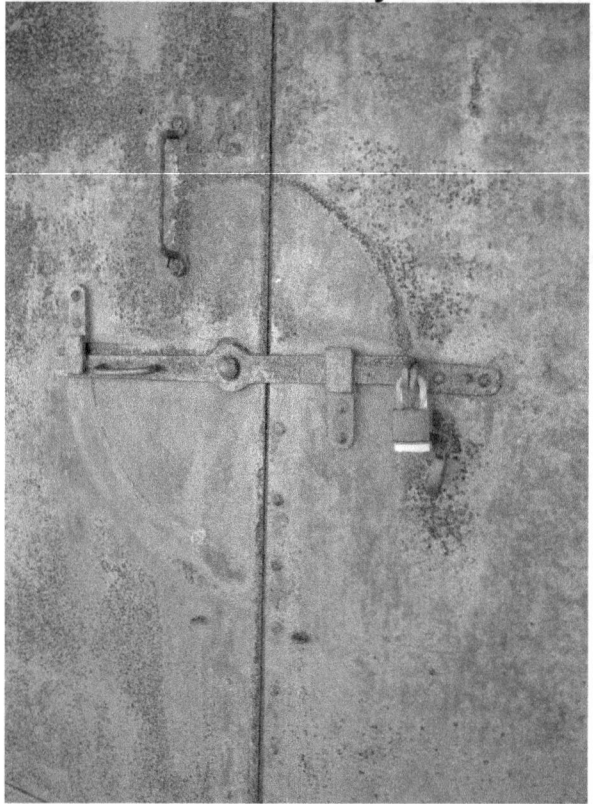

How much we share of our lives is our choice.
We all know how sad and lonely it feels to be left out, but it is equally heartbreaking to refuse to let others in.
We all need to feel loved and accepted.

We all benefit in sharing our lives and love with others.
Offer your friendship to someone. You might just be the one thing they need. More surprising, you might find it is the one thing you need.
Show a bit of compassion to someone.
Accept a gesture of generosity offered to you.
Soften your heart. Take a chance. Your life will be richer.
Show Us Who You Are
The real you is dying to burst through the clouds.
You have much to offer the world.
Break through; show the world your stuff.
Don't be afraid; don't worry about being accepted.
It's time to stop trying to impress others with a false persona.
The time has come to make an impact on the world with the real you.
You are astonishing just as you are; you brighten the world.
You shine like there is no tomorrow.
Push your way through; live for today.
The real you is bigger than life.
Stop hiding and let the world see you.
Touch the world, warm hearts radiate with all your might.

Wading in the Creek:
Are you secretive?
Do you feel included in daily life?
Do you make friends easily?
Do you like being with a group of people or do you prefer being alone?
Do you worry about being accepted by others?

Swimming the River:

Write a character sketch of someone you consider to be an open book.
Write a personal narrative that includes this line "I knew they were talking about me…"
Write a scene involving an insecure person.
Write a short story about someone showing off.
Write a poem titled "Astonish".

Come On In

No one need invite you to live your life. It is your destination.

Do you need an invitation to life?
The gate is open. Come on in.
If you must, swing on the gate first.
You might just find it's the best ride you've ever had.
The other side might be even better than where you've been.
There are places to go and people to meet.

There are dreams to chase.
You'll never do those things if you don't accept the call.
Life is waiting for you.
Stop hanging in the shadows and let the sun shine upon your face.
Let your soul awaken and allow your heart to speak; give yourself a chance
to discover and fulfill your purpose.
Surrender yourself and let life lead you by the hand.
Aren't you itching to find out what is waiting for you?
Don't let fear hold you back.
Own your thoughts. Own your actions. Own your life.
No one else is quite like you.
If you do not live your life, who will?

Wading in the Creek:
Are you a person who takes initiative?
Do you plan your days?
Does spontaneity frighten you?
Why do you or do you not chase dreams?
Is life waiting on you or are you waiting on life.

Swimming the River:
Write a personal narrative about not being invited to something you desperately wanted to attend.
Write scene of someone denying his/her "calling".
Write about an unusual event in your life. (Examples: You went somewhere you never thought you'd go, or you did something on a dare.)
Write a story that includes this "…as I hesitated to knock he opened the door."
Write a poem titled "Here I am".

PART TWO

SELF-TRUST AND RESPONSIBILITY

When you fully love and accept yourself you are able to love and accept others without expectation. Having an honest relationship with yourself is a primary step to developing deeper relationships with others.

Using and Abusing Personal Power

Everyone can do a world of good by doing good in the world.

Every interaction, no matter how great or small, is an exchange of power. We feed positively or negatively off one another. We can lift one another up or take them down with us.

Every single thing we do has a motive, good or bad, behind it. We have a reason behind every action we take whether it is in our own self-interest or not. Sometimes doing good for others is still a selfish motive; yet it is not harmful as opposed to intentionally hurting those around us.

Performing from a place of love sets good things in motion. When our intentions are based in love, everyone's best interest is at the heart of the matter. There is no room for jealousy, greed, fear, or hatred in the realm of love.

Most people can be categorized into givers or takers. Manipulators give in order to take. They act out of their own insecurities and fears. Many of us do things for others all the time; we might do it simply because they need our assistance. We might even get personal satisfaction knowing we are needed. There are times we do things for material gain. Other times we do things for personal empowerment such as being able to manipulate or control their actions by guilting them to owe us something.

When we make choices at the detriment of another's emotional or physical well-being we've crossed the line. When we gain materially or emotionally at another's loss we've not only robbed them but ourselves as well. The gain is short lived because anyone who has a healthy sense of right and wrong will eventually come to know the extent of what has been done. Who does not feel guilty in the long run when they realize the pain they've caused to others? When we do things out of love without motive, there's no need to explain our actions. When we remind people how much we do for others, possibly our own conscience is trying to awaken us to the reality of our intentions. When we bring attention to the things we do, it's time to examine our own motives. Those who use power to control another's life or influence them to side with them on the matter at hand are acting out of fear. It takes courage to remain quiet and let the situation play itself out. Good deeds need no explanation as they speak for themselves.

When we help others do we establish that something must be done in return for our favor? When we serve unselfishly and the time comes we need assistance, faith guarantees us love and compassion will be returned to us.

None of us need allow another to control us. They have nothing of internal value we need in this life. All we need rests within us. We only need look inside for guidance. We each have a lifetime supply of love. With love as our motive we will always win.

Wading in the Creek:

What has happened when you have acted with a selfish motive?

When have you acted purely in the self-interest of another person?

How have you managed to resolve a situation for the best of all involved?

Where have you been able to fit time for service to others in your lifestyle?

What has been the greatest blessing in your life stemming from an act of service?

Swimming the River:

Write about the most selfish act you've ever witnessed.

Write a personal narrative/memoir about a selfless act.

Write a dramatic monologue concerning personal power.

Write a poem (any style) depicting your energy as wind.

Write a scene where two people want the same thing but for different reasons.

Laws of Nature

We should never give less than what we expect in return.

We attract what we emit. Treat the world with compassion.

What we give is what we are returned. Be a friend to others.

Do all you do in the name of love and you will be blessed with love.

Deal in honesty. Others will trust you and be open with you.

Show others you care and they will care for you.
Express an attitude of gratitude. Grace will follow.
Be forgiving. Others will extend mercy to you.
Trust others enough to extend opportunities to them
and the same will come to you.
Teach your talents to those willing to learn and listen
to those willing to teach you. It will all come full circle.
Accept others as they are without forcing your
opinions on them. They will accept and respect you
as you are.
Be kind and gentle. Those of the same disposition will
find their way to you.
Be giving. Help others. When the need arises, others
will be there for you.
Be responsible and accountable. People will depend
on you, but they will also hold themselves liable to
their actions.
Look for the good in those you meet. They will also
see the good in you.
Always do your best. Those around you will expend
their best efforts as well.
Seek to be a comfort in the weariness of the world.
Peace comes to those who live their lives in harmony
with others.

Wading in the Creek:
How has being honest in a tough situation paid off for
you?
When has someone given you the benefit of the
doubt?
Has someone ever trusted you in circumstances you
were hesitant to trust yourself?
Have you ever been forgiven when you felt you did
not deserve mercy?
What act of kindness bestowed upon you has had the
greatest impact on your life?

Swimming the River:

Write about something you have done for a complete stranger or about something done for you by someone you didn't know.

Write a ballad involving the laws of attraction.

Write about someone you feel was placed in your life for a specific reason.

Write a story involving the act of forgiveness.

Rewrite the story where forgiveness isn't granted.

Into the Blue

Never be too busy to rest in the now.

Ever feel a bit melancholy, not all out depressed but just need to recharge your batteries? Do you take the time to do it?

When you catch yourself drifting into the cool and calm of the blue zone do you snap back to reality or enjoy it for a while?

At some time or another, most of us feel the need to take a time out. We desire to rest, reassess, refocus, and reenergize.

We learn a lot when we do this. We see what motivates others and how they interact. We recognize patterns of our own cravings in life and how those affect others.

We track our own progress in problem identification and solving. We look at where we've been and assess where we are to help us determine where we want to go. When we reflect we begin to know ourselves on a deeper level.

When you're feeling stressed, run down, or overwhelmed, don't hesitate to pull out the time out chair and sit a spell. It does wonders for the soul. Watching the world pass you by for just a bit is soothing...just be sure to slide off the chair and jump back into life.

Wading in the Creek:
How do you transition into reality after vacation?
In what ways has your life been affected by depression?
What relaxation techniques help you focus?
What have you learned about yourself by reflecting on your life?
Are your personal needs met more fully in solitude or in a group setting?

Swimming the River:

Write a persuasive argument on the benefits of being an extrovert or an introvert.

Write a short story about someone being so exhausted he/she can't get out of bed. Throw in an unusual twist to get them up.

Write a character sketch for a girl named Melancholy. What might she look like? How might she act? Include a setting of her surroundings to support her name.

Write a poem about "running on empty".

Write a scene depicting character traits of an overworked person and a hyperactive friend.

A Search for Self

You know who you are. Don't be afraid to share yourself with the world.

Who Am I?

This is the universal question we all wander around and wonder about. Only the brave and diligent find the answer, and even then the answer is as ever changing as time itself.

You cannot find yourself by looking through the eyes of your family or friends. You must search within yourself. You must probe where the eyes can't see. You must be brave enough to allow your heart to lead the way. You must be willing to make the journey. Yes, I said journey. This simple question often involves a long complex passage before it is answered.

We often come to this question when we feel a void in our lives. It is human nature to look outside ourselves to find ourselves. We usually look for something larger than ourselves to fill the void. Some look for God, and others first try to fill that void with things. It might be material things, or substances which numb the ache within us. There are numerous addictions (alcohol, drugs, sex, gambling) people turn to avoid facing themselves all while the answers rest within.

If you have a true desire to know yourself, approach with passion and purpose. Looking deep inside one will find that sacred place, that core where spirituality begins. Finding this place is the beginning of filling the void. Somewhere in that realm you will find yourself. Before diving into self, we sometimes set high expectations which result in disappointment. We have to remember searching the self is not like spending a day at the office. Poking at your soul can make you feel unpleasant and bring about more questions than answers. Emotions and memories will be stirred up, tossed about, and thrown in our faces. It is not a pantry filled with labels, cans, and boxes. It is often found to be a disorganized closet crammed with articles not relating to one another. It can be overwhelming trying to make sense of the mess. We might feel out of control and naturally want to shut down. Never lose hope. The light is there. It is beckoning you. Peel the layers back one at a time. It will get brighter and brighter as you continue. Are you beginning to see the light?

The power is yours. No one else can tell you who you are. The key to your identity, your peace, and your happiness is the same. It all rests in authenticity. The answers remain within you until you pull them out.

Wading in the Creek:
How have you managed to fill the void in your life?
How has answering some questions led you to even greater truths?
How is the person others expect you to be different than the one who lives within you?
Does your happiness depend on outside sources or do you have a peace that resides within you?
In what ways do you like or dislike the person you think you are?

Swimming the River:
Write a story about finding something.
Write a personal narrative/memoir about a time of confusion. Take us through the discovery process, one layer at a time.
Describe a disorganized business setting. Give attention to detail.
Write a scene centering on a character who suffers from dementia or amnesia.
Write a poem titled "Lost".

Feeding the Beast Within

When you move where you fear to tread the beast within settles in for the night.

We are all hungry beasts. We hunger for success. We hunger to be heard. We hunger to be known.

Yet, we are gentle giants. We hold back in fear. We fear failure. We fear ridicule. We fear we will be misunderstood.

Fear is an obstacle because we let it grow out of hand. We allow it to consume us. When we reel in our imagination the fears shrink.

Are we afraid of our own power? Obligation comes with power. Possibility arises with power. When we tap into our source our lives change. Feeding the hunger does not mean losing control. It means making choices and adapting to change. It provides us with an opportunity for growth.

Hunger is painful, but fear is immobilizing. How will you feed the beasts within?

Wading in the Creek:

What do you hunger most for in life?

How do you feed the hungry beast within you?

Why do you think most of us are afraid of our own power?

Are you held back more by the possibility of failure or success?

Why do you feel it is important to be understood?

Swimming the River:

Write a story about someone who constantly eats.

Write a café scene. How are people interacting?

What do they see, hear, smell, or taste?

Write a character sketch of a person who can't satisfy his/her hunger. What is his/her physical appearance and habits?

Write a personal narrative/memoir about overindulging in food or drink.

Write a poem titled Hunger.

Flower or Thorn?

Your character will be revealed by your ability to use your gifts and the choices you make. Will you bloom your way into the world or poke your way through?

We are each gifted with both the blossom and the spikes. Which we choose to use creates our lives. We may use our blossoms to delight the eye or soothe the soul. Some prefer to look pretty with little concern for others. Some choose to spend their time making others feel better.

We use our thorns as a protective layer to keep others from getting close and penetrating the surface. We protect our space and our property. We look out for ourselves.

There are times we jab others for no reason at all. We might be having a bad day, feeling ill, or just not getting our way when we want. When we choose this route, we are being selfish and hurtful. Are we even aware when we do this? Does it really make us feel any better? When we put our own wants and needs above others, making ourselves seem of more importance, what does it really say about us? We are all guilty of this at one time or another whether we admit it or not.

When someone else pokes us, how we react says more about us than about the person inflicting the pain. I've had my days of reacting in anger, pain, and frustration. I've called names, yelled, and held grudges. Sometimes I've apologized for my behavior, other times not. We expect to be forgiven whether asked to be or not. And sometimes we choose to remain silent. It doesn't lessen the pain, but it prevents escalating a situation that never should have been created.

We can allow our petals to unfurl, offering kindness and generosity. We can let our lives blossom with love. Or we can prick and snarl at others, hurting them and ourselves in the process. Do we really want to wither spirits, our own included?

So, who are you, the flower or the thorn? You decide. We are all students of life. Occasionally, we get to be the teacher. And sometimes we are merely the lesson.

Wading in the Creek:

Do you tend to use your blossoms or thorns to get your way?
Do you have difficulty allowing people to get close to you?
How do you allow your moods to affect those around you?
Are you confrontational?
How do you look for lessons in the mist of disappointment?

Swimming the River:

Write a rosebush dialogue. Present the thorns and blooms at odds with one another.
Write a poem containing the words unfurl, time, thorn, and wall.
Write a story about someone who has taken a vow of silence. Does he/she break it? Why or why not?
Write about a time you chose to remain silent on an issue. What were your motives? What did you accomplish?
Write about a time someone called you out on your behavior. Did the situation escalate or resolve? Did the confrontation anger you?

Be the Sun

When you create sunshine in the lives of others you warm your own soul in the process.

You can be the sun.
Stop hiding beneath those clouds.
Do your own thing.
Shine for all to see.
You are bright and vibrant, a shining force in this time.
Radiate. Expand. Help those around you grow.
Be larger than life.
Be the shining star you were born to be.
Be the bright intruder who chases away the darkness.
Just being you will bring a smile to others.
Just being you will give you peace.
May the path you travel be wide and the lives you touch be warmed.
Rise and shine. Be the sun.

Wading in the Creek:
Do you tend to hide in the shadows of others?
When do you demand the spotlight?
Have you accomplished the things you think you were meant to do?
Why do you think others enjoy being around you?
What is your gift to the world?

Swimming the River:
Write a personal narrative about doing your thing.
Write a poem about "being".
Write a story about the "brightest thing I/he/she ever saw".
Detail a setting with lots of shadows. How is this place scary or not? What types of things happen here?
Write a scene where two people spot a shiny object in the grass.

Obstructions in the Forest of Life

What some call impossibilities might merely be challenges.

Many of us trudge through life while others charge full steam ahead. We can be mindlessly going about our way when suddenly we are faced with an obstacle. It can be of our own making or created by someone else. We face physical and emotional obstacles. Regardless, we must choose how we deal with it. Do we remove it or find a way over it or around it?
There might be times we can slide beneath it and continue. Other times we might get stuck beneath its weight while trying. Perhaps we clear it, but still carry a bit of the burden with us.
There are times jumping over might not be as difficult as we think. Then again, we might stumble in the process. It might be just that, a stop on the journey.

There are even times we feel so energetic and powerful we barge right through obstacles with no repercussions. Other times the effects linger.

There are times we must reroute, walk around it, or even pretend it doesn't exist. Some

It might simply be a crossroad forcing us to make a choice. These choices can be the most painful steps of all.

There are times we are at a standstill and unable to do anything. When it happens we are thankful for those who hold us up. Obstacles can make us face truths in life we've never had the courage to confront.

Wading in the Creek:

Why do you think obstacles appear out of nowhere?

Do you look for a lesson in the situation or just try to work through it?

Has anything ever put you at a standstill, physically or emotionally?

What truths have thrown you for a loop?

How has an obstruction in your path enriched your life?

Swimming the River:

Write a personal narrative/memoir about a change in plans.

Write a dialogue between siblings disputing the care for an elderly parent.

Write a story using an obstruction as a life lesson. Have your setting help drive home the lesson.

Write a story about a tree or boulder cutting off the entrance/exit to a village. Tell how the villagers work together to remove it or rebuild the road around it.

Who Paints Your Picture Perfectly?

You are the artist of your world. You choose the scenery and the colors. Make your picture one of peace and joy.

Water runs across the earth. The ground reaches into the sky. Colors blend and burst forth into life.
Elements work together to give and sustain life.
Nature creates a perfect picture at times.
Sometimes our lives seem picture perfect as well. We appear healthy, happy, and financially sound. Are our work, family, and social lives balanced?
To whom does this picture look perfect? To us or outsiders? Did we collaborate with others to create this picture? Is it our dream or someone else's?
Did we paint this picture or just somehow end up as part of the scenery? Is it the life we want or have chosen?

What is ideal anyway? Does it depend on how we were raised? Where we grew up? Where we currently live? Our religion? Our finances? Our occupation? How we dress? Our moral ethics?
Who sets the goals of achievement? Each of our ideas of success varies.
Who determines what constitutes balance in a life? We each need different things to ground us and to motivate us.
Does picture perfect equal being healthy, happy, and at peace?
Do you let others set the criteria for your life or do you set your own?
Are your expectations reasonable and attainable?
How do you define success?
Have you achieved balance in your life?

Wading in the Creek:
Do you feel peace in all areas of your life?
Are you a daydreamer?
What's missing in your life?
Why do you feel it is or is not perfect?
When are you least reasonable in your expectations?

Swimming the River:
Write a personal narrative/memoir about a moment of success.
Write a short story about a family's expectations of one another. Are they reasonable or far-fetched? What problems arise because of these expectations?
Write a poem about rational.
Draw a character sketch of yourself as one of nature's elements. What do you look like? How do you act? Do you have a nickname?
Describe a setting of perfection.

The Complexity of Happiness, Plain and Simple

Happiness grows on trees of good intention. Aim to do your best and the rest follows.

What is happiness? Is it the lack of sadness? Is it some preconceived notion we've heard from someone else? Do we consider ourselves happy when we reach all the goals someone else sets before us? Are we happy when we are free of debt? Employed? Successful at our careers? Does happiness depend on good health, companionship, or financial security?

Does being happy mean that life will no longer have difficult moments? Or does it simply mean that we have attained the skills to survive setbacks?

Does being happy mean we fear nothing and no one disagrees with us? Or does it simply mean we are willing to take risks and are accepting of what is different from us?

Does being happy mean we're overjoyed every minute of every day? Or does it simply mean that we have learned to find gratitude with the familiar?

Is happiness taking responsibility for our choices, actions, and feelings?

Could happiness truly just be peace of mind and heart? A lack of worry? Could it simply be awareness and acceptance of the moment, and the ability to find comfort in the here and now?

Many consider happiness to be obtained only by wealth or sacrifice. Can it not be considered a value? After all, we are all given the basic right to pursue it. It is available. It's a matter of looking in the right place for it. Do we know where happiness thrives?

Is happiness an opportunity, a destination, or a way of living?

Wading in the Creek:
Are you happy more often than sad?
What makes you sad?
When do you feel happiest?
Does your happiness depend on other people's successes or failures?
Does your definition of happiness differ from your friends and family?

Swimming the River:

Write about a time you felt happier than you've ever felt? Was it because of the people you were with? Was it an accomplishment? Was it something relatively simple that filled your heart?

Write an essay defining happiness through the generations of your family.

Think about all the things that simplify your life. Write about how you could still be happy without those things.

Write a story about someone who tries to buy happiness.

Write a poem about where happiness lives.

Merit of Self-maintenance

Never feel beyond repair. New blessings arise with the sun each morning.

Sometimes we break. We chip, dent, or are in desperate need of repair. We might be aware of our faults and fallacies, or we might not have a clue. Some of us might not even care. Perhaps the people we associate with hammer us into the shape we are in. Maybe we've been on a self-destructive course. Time wears and tears us; perhaps all we need is a bit of glue and a little polishing.

There are days we feel worn, rusty, outdated, overlooked or underappreciated. We think we're being victimized. And then again, if we take a closer look we might find we are our own demise. Sometimes an adjustment of attitude makes all the difference.

There are times we can't find our way in. We lock ourselves out. We lose the key. We reinforce our gates. We expect others to repair us when we aren't willing to do the work ourselves. We forget we still hold the key even if it seems invisible.

Other times we don't see the whole picture. It's possible we are perfect just the way we are. Just because we don't realize our own importance or purpose does not mean it doesn't exist. We do exist, and we are important. None of us are without purpose. We usually depend on others to tell us. We often fail to remember how necessary it is for us to tell it to ourselves.

Wading in the Creek:
What do you feel you need to work on in your life?
When have you felt unappreciated?
Are you able to reassure yourself when you are feeling down?
How do you "maintain" yourself?
Do you depend on others to validate you?

Swimming the River:
Write about a time you didn't see the whole picture until after you did something you shouldn't have done.
Write a poem about "maintenance".
Write a scene where one person sees the full picture and the other is clueless.
Write a character sketch of someone who only sees what affects him.
Write a setting of a building in disrepair on the outside yet beautiful on the inside. What might be happening in this building?

The Waiting Game

If you push your way through life you might miss what was waiting for you all along.

I spent my life waiting. It seemed like forever.
I was a late bloomer. Life was difficult being a bud among blossoms.
I only wanted to be one of "them". I thought my time would never come.
Little did I know I needed to accept myself for others to accept me.
I was not writing my own story, and I didn't know where to begin.

I yearned for acceptance. I just wanted to fit in.
If I couldn't be one of the roses, why couldn't I be a rare orchid?
I was neither, but I managed to blend in by becoming who I thought they wanted me to be.
I played the character I thought written for me and became part of their story.
I ran away from myself time after time. I stood outside of my life waiting for an invitation to participate in it.
While I was afraid of being considered different, I equally feared finding out I wasn't so unique after all.
Life continued to take me down many paths of waiting, wandering, and wondering.
Eventually, I met myself head on.
I know I am right where I belong. I am writing my story as I live it, and I've made myself the main character.
It's time for you to stop waiting for other to tell you of your worth. It's time for you to show your value.
Set your own standards. Be who you are and in your time.

Wading in the Creek:
Have you ever waited a long time for something?
Are you a patient waiter?
Are you a clock counter or a calendar marker?
Why do you concern yourself about other's standards of time?
What makes you feel you are or are not right where you should be?

Swimming the River:
Write a personal narrative/memoir about a rite of passage.
Write a character driven story. Show an extreme difference between his personal and public personas.
Write a poem reflecting "Who I am not".

Write a story with most things in the setting of similar likeness except one vastly different thing. Show how this difference can create conflict or interest among your characters.
Detail a character unlike her friends and family. How does she impact those around her and vice versa?

Work in Progress

Every season of life is as important as the one you've passed through and the one you're headed into. This moment right now is where you are; don't let it pass you by.

Every stage in life is just as important as the last or the next.
We learn. We grow. We evolve. Life is a process.
Our lives are what we make of it. Where we go is up to us.

We are not here by chance.
We are intentions cast into a world of possibilities.
Some purposes are clearer than others.
We might ease our way through the world,
We might know exactly what we're here to do.
As we soak life in we expand.
We can sit and wait for life to come for us.
Or we can use what we've been gifted.
We can choose to fly.

Wading in the Creek:
Do you know your life purpose?
Do you have a career goal?
How have you prepared yourself to reach these goals?
Are you a high achiever?
Do you dream more than you prepare for life?

Swimming the River:
Write a story about a person with (metaphorical or physical) wings.
Write a poem titled "The Gift".
Write a character outline of someone with vision.
Remember the importance of minute details.
Write a story with a main character struggling between a career and a calling.
Write a scene involving someone who is feeling his way through life.

Stepping Stones across the Creek

We will be taught the same lesson many times and in many ways throughout our lives. Perhaps we'll eventually learn it.

The creek was literally the property line where I grew up. I spent my days crossing the creek to get to my cousin's house. I could either traverse by rocks where the water flowed over the dirt road, or I could steady myself across a makeshift bridge positioned between both creek banks.

Throughout my lifetime I've crossed the creek many times. I've waded through the water, jumped from rock to rock, and even straddled logs to get from bank to bank. Sometimes I've fallen in and other times I've cleared the water. Every time I got wet I came up with a new strategy for crossing the next time. It could have been adding bigger rocks or placing them closer together. I may have even just needed to steady myself before taking that first step. But always, I tried just one more time. Practice really does make perfect; well maybe not perfect, but possible.

Metaphorically speaking, I've had to cross many rocks along the creek that runs through my life. Insecurity has been a hard rock to jump over. It has taken me many attempts to trust myself. My gut instinct is almost always on target, yet I struggle to believe I know what I am doing or where I am going. I have never quite felt safe. I always thought everything and everyone was bigger and better than me. Though I craved security, I never realized that I had often been the obstacle in my own path. Only through reflection have I recently realized I've always had available the tools I needed for self-growth. Why was I afraid to use them?

This brings me to the rock of fear. I have grown up emotionally afraid of almost everything unfamiliar to me. I lacked courage in many ways. I probably would have done a better job if I'd closed my eyes and not seen where I was going. Vision is what caused my fear. Once I saw what was in front of me, my thought process took over and paralyzed me. Had I felt my way across the creek, I'd have gotten to the other side much quicker.

Perhaps it was not only vision but lack of trust in my own abilities that immobilized me. Eventually, I found the courage to rationalize and trust myself. In trusting I learned it was ok to get wet.

I was once in a place of sadness. I didn't know that most of it stemmed from selfishness. I was focused on myself and how others affected me. I didn't examine how my actions and reactions affected them. I doubted my value to others. I lived wanting the world to change, not knowing that simply altering my own heart would shift my small world. I removed myself as a victim in my world and began to live victoriously. I instilled generosity into my life. Joy, peace, and harmony naturally followed, and my life began to take on new meaning.

The most difficult rock for me to step across was anxiety. My life was based on apprehension. I was a bundle of nervous energy waiting for the world around me to collapse. I had to retrain my thought process and adjust my view. I had to stop thinking about what could happen. I had to stop worrying about the future and start living in the present. I had to learn to focus on the positive aspects of life and let go of negativity. This was the most important step I've ever taken. It was life changing. This very process led me to an inner peace I never knew existed.

Many times I've rearranged the rocks in my life. I've rebuilt dams, piled rocks higher in certain areas and removed them all together in other spaces. The result has been freely flowing water with the creation of lovely falls. My dam is stronger in some places and needs continuous reinforcement, but such is life. It is ever constant and ever changing, but beautiful all the same.

Wading in the Creek:
What rock do you find yourself crossing continuously?
Do you find it difficult to let go of doubt?
Have you found focusing on the positive helpful to you?
Have you ever considered yourself a victim of life or circumstance?
How has anxiety played into your decision making?
Construct a "found" poem as one would build a dam.

Swimming the River:

Write a story about a failing (physical or metaphorical) dam.

Write a personal narrative about a time you had to shift your attitude.

Create a character and detail him as a bundle of nervous energy.

Write a dialogue between two selfish people who want something done their way and refuses to relent.

Write a scene of someone falling in the water.

Beauty Within

You are a whisper of splendor that graces the world.

When we hear the word beauty, we think of things we see. We think of beauty as we are conditioned to perceive it. Few of us consider ourselves to be beautiful. We forget not all beauty is visual.

If we look beneath the surface we see beauty everywhere. We paint the world in rainbows of love, generosity, and kindness. Beauty is found within us. A thing standing alone might seem simple, but placed with other things can become an expansive view, beauty you actually inhale. You feel the sacred in your bones. The breath of life brushes against your skin as you become a dot of paint on the painter's canvas. We live within a moment of beauty.

We are confronted by beauty every day; beauty that is ordinary. We take it for granted. We fail to see the extent of something quite so extraordinary because our own perception is distorted by the conditions of daily living.

Often we hear beauty speak in the silence around us. It is a state of being. It drifts across the sky, rains upon the earth, and springs forth in new life. Beauty rests in possibility. It is the hope of what is to come. Beauty powers all that ever was and what it is ever changing to be. It whispers to us and calms us but has the power to pull us under. So while they claim beauty to be a seductress, it is actually a sustainer. Beauty is relative.

Beauty emerges when we think all usefulness is gone. We know what was given, what was sacrificed, and what was birthed because of it. Petals fall and fuzzy tendrils catch the tail of the wind. They touch down here and there and the world becomes a better place. We can be the beauty that caresses the earth. If we don't clearly identify beauty, we think it is hidden, perhaps beneath stone. Or we think that maybe it doesn't exist at all. Though beauty can't always be seen, we know it's there when we feel it. Nothing short of beautiful can make us feel loved, full of life, and hopeful for the future. Simply, beauty is a combination of belief and trust.

Wading in the Creek:
How do you define beauty?
Where is the most unlikely place you have found beauty?
When have you found beauty at the root of tragedy?
Why do you feel we focus on outer beauty more than inner beauty?
How have you taken the beauty of your own circumstances for granted?

Swimming the River:
Using only concrete nouns and verbs, no adjectives or adverbs, create a setting of beauty. Experiment with the use of simile and metaphor.
Write a poem about emerging beauty.
Write a story with "it/he/she took my breath away".
Write a personal narrative/memoir about a piece of clothing and its beauty or seductive nature.
Write a marriage proposal to your significant other relaying all the beauty he/she exudes. This can be a fictional piece as well.

Getting Through the Thick of It

When we learn to function in the fog, we will never fear the darkness.

There are times we seem to exist in a fog of mental clarity. The stresses of life cloud our visibility. We might be so bogged down by the past that our current reality ceases to exist. We might be so focused on memories that we neglect to see what is right in front of us. We seclude ourselves to the point that only memories can touch us. We become lost in a haze. Sometimes we need to reject the redundant so that we may see the essential.

There are also times we live in a fog of indecision or uncertainty. We feel restless and our lives have little or no direction. It is as if we are caught in the midst of contradiction. As much as we dislike it being uncomfortable can move us to action. It pushes us to regain our power and confidence. Sometimes, we just need to give the fog time to lift and we find that the answers were within us all along.

We can search so deeply for truth that we are swallowed by our own doubt. We grasp for meaning within the confusion. Life loses color, and we live in shades of gray. It can be at that point of internal discomfort the light of truth filters into our being. The power of truth illuminates the fog surrounding us. Truth helps us to see more clearly.

There are times we don't find answers or truth. Nor do we find directions or instructions. We can either grasp our way in the fog or refocus our energies in other things. When we reach through the thickness to those we love and expect to support us, their advice might really of no consequence to us. It might simply be enough for them to listen, acknowledge, and love us back. We need to remember we travel in circles so we will come around. As we let the mist settle into our skin, we will find ourselves.

Wading in the Creek:
Do you ever feel foggy headed?
What activities clear your head?
When has being uncomfortable about something moved you to action?
Is it easy for you to refocus your energy?
How does uncertainty affect you?

Swimming the River:
Write a dialogue between a boat captain and passengers as they travel through foggy waters.
Write a scene of something coming into view as fog rises. Be sure to play up your setting.
Write a poem about contradiction.
Write a personal narrative/memoir about indecision.
Write a story about someone living in a mental fog.

As We Journey through Time

We reach our destination much quicker when we trust the journey.

It is seldom that life is an even playing field. We generally have peaks and valleys to cross, rivers to swim, and mountains to climb to get exactly where we want to be. Of course, life is what we make it. We all have different priorities and different roads to travel to our destinations. It helps to stop and take in the view along the way to be appreciative of our current circumstances.

We usually come upon curves on the road of life. Swamp and rivers can keep us from reaching the place we want to be. We have the power to build bridges to cross over to our promised land.

There will be times we feel like we are zigzagging through life. Not really going up or down, just trudging in and out. We feel like we're getting nowhere fast. If we look hard enough we might find some flowers along the way. There might even be a lesson tucked beneath a rock. We might not be aware of why we feel stagnant, and only on looking back will we see wisdom in the trail.

Sometimes we have a simple yet sturdy set of stairs within us. We climb to the top and it's exactly where we want to be. Maybe it was meticulous planning on our part or maybe someone came before us and laid it out ahead of time. Maybe we are following the steps of those taken before us. Whatever the reason, things just fall into place.

The pursuit of whatever we are looking can be a steep and treacherous climb. We might feel overwhelmed or even defeated, but it's important to just keep trying because it's usually only temporary. We most often find our goal is not as far away or as difficult to achieve as we anticipated it to be.

When the destination is in sight, hope returns. Our strength soars. A little hope can reenergize us to complete the task before us.

When we reach the intended point, we feel a sense of freedom. We find having the faith to go the distance was really what the journey was all about anyway. Sometimes, truth stands alone, but there is no greater peace than having traveled long enough to find a place to settle down with happiness.

Wading in the Creek:

In reflection have you found your journeys or destinations to be the most rewarding?

Do you feel like you are more often on your way somewhere or enjoying the point you've reached?

Are you too focused on your destination to notice the scenery?

Do you feel more joy or relief when you reach a goal?

Do you depend more on faith or plans to get you where you are going?

Swimming the River:

Write a poem "On the way".

Write a personal narrative/memoir about a getting lost on a trip.

Write a scene of pedestrian pursuing a thief.

Write a story of a treacherous climb. Be creative in what you are climbing and why.

Write a dialogue between the roadside scenery and a weary traveler.

The Weeping Soul

It takes great courage to continue the race when we want to give up. When we keep going we find winning was never the goal. It is about completing the task and what we learn in the process. Yes, it's all about living, reigniting the soul.

A weeping soul is often a wandering soul, for it is restless.
It seldom sits still.

It doesn't stay around long enough to become attached.
It has found love hurts too much.
Rather than take a chance, it runs.
The weeping soul must learn to trust, itself and others.
When the weeping soul discovers courage, it can forgive itself.
When it opens the door to forgiveness, it will find love and happiness are right around the corner.
When the weeping soul learns to share its tears and laughter with the world, it will truly be free.
When the weeping soul lets go of the past, it will live again.

Wading in the Creek:
Do you consider yourself to be a trusting?
Are you a wanderer?
Do you cry for times gone by?
Why are you or are you not courageous?
Do you feel happy right now?

Swimming the River:
Write a personal narrative/memoir about not being able to stop crying.
Write a poem about a Weeping Willow.
Write a story about a wandering soul. Is this soul a person? Where is it wandering? What is it searching for?
Write a dialogue between courage and forgiveness.
Write a scene showing of an underground spring reaching the surface. Tell why the earth is crying.

The Sun Shines Within Our Souls

Often a quiet resolve is all that's needed to acquire the wisdom of life.

Even when we fail to feel the sun shining on our backs, it is still in the background trying to light our way and hoping to warm our lives.
We tend to look to others for guidance when we have a heart that will happily show us the way.
We look to the world for wisdom when our souls contain the knowledge of life.
When we feel despondent it's good to remember all we really need is within our reach. We often think we

need certain things, and are frustrated when we they seem to be out of our grasp.

We tend to think we know what is best for us.

Perhaps when things pass us by, it is because something better is waiting around the corner.

When we learn to be still, peace comes to us.

When we learn to be quiet, we listen.

When we listen, we can hear that voice within speak to us.

When we trust ourselves, we find freedom.

When we are free, there's nothing we can't accomplish.

Remember whether we see the sun or not, it is always there.

Wading in the Creek:

Do you focus on the positivity of bad situations?

Do you always seem to be wanting for more or are you fairly content?

What time of the day is your quiet time?

Do you accomplish most things you set out to do?

Do you generally heed the voice within?

Swimming the River:

Write a story about the "knowledge of life".

Write a poem titled "Still".

Write an essay comparing hope to sunshine. How are they alike? How are they different? Do they feel similar?

Write about a time you were upset by not getting what you wanted only to find something better was waiting for you.

Write about a time you heard your soul speak. What did it sound like? What did it tell you to do? Did you follow its instructions? What happened? Include dialogue.

Corridors of Life

When you hide beneath your shadow you cease to see the light.

As we walk through the corridors of life, boards creak and shadows linger. When we find the source of creaks and see the shadows for what they are, we find they aren't obstacles at all. They are merely substance along the journey; things that make us stop and think before we continue. Reevaluate the situation if needed. If not appreciate the moment for what it us.
We are not promised a clear passageway. We are gifted life, but breathing is up to us. Chances are if we

stumble we can be assured someone will lift us up. Even so, we must exercise our strength to know we are capable.

There will be lights to guide us and beams to hold us up. We must find it within ourselves to trust the light and build a support system.

When we listen we find the heartbeat and footsteps we hear belong to us. The shadows are the fears we've cast upon our lives, and most importantly the door we see ahead might be the one we're supposed to walk through. If we are not meant to walk that way we will come upon another door. Mistakes are not the end of the road. Failures are bumps of experience along the journey.

Life is obscure. Time is uncertain. Know shadows cannot exist without a source of light, and neither can we.

Look deep. Find your source. Continue the walk.

Wading in the Creek:

Do you take time to think your way out of a situation or do you continue blindly?

Why do you feel obstacles are sometimes thrown in your path?

Why do you feel you are more shadow or light?

Are you a good listener?

Do you usually see things clearly or the way you want to see them?

Swimming the River:

Write a scene of two people passing in a corridor of an old historical building.

Write about a time of your life you now view as a passageway to your current life.

Write a story about the longest hallway ever.

Write a scene involving an unknown passageway.

Write a poem using the words shadow, creak,
stumble, and flicker.

PART THREE

RELATIONSHIP WITH SELF AND WITH OTHERS

An important step of personal empowerment is having the courage to trust your instincts. You respect yourself and others by allowing yourself to be accountable for your thoughts and actions.

Peeking Through the Trees

When we stop judging every outcome as failure or triumph and view it as experience, decisions and compromise become easier to make.

We often only peek through the curtains of life.
We are afraid to open them wide and let the world in.
We hide in the shadows and catch glimpses now and then.
Maybe we're afraid we will see the truth, the truth of those around us.
Possibly we don't want to see the situation for what it is.
Or perhaps, we don't want to face our own truth.
Life is not always ideal. We don't always get our way.
Health issues arise. We lose jobs. We argue with friends. Nastiness lurks in the corridors, temptation

lingers, tempers flare, and obstacles attack us head on. We will always struggle from time to time.
It is what we take from the struggle that is most important, that being the choices we make.
Compromise is inevitable.
How we arrive at that compromise is where truth is exposed. Power is used and abused. Sacrifices are made. Character is revealed.
As a result our lives change. How we handle transition tells our story.
Do we keep our integrity intact? Do we make decisions at the cost of others?
We might prefer to avoid the nastiness and drama and see the good in all. While it is right to focus on the positives of life, sometimes we have to face the nature of things.
We have to stare the ugly truth in the face.
Sometimes things are not at all as they seem.
In those times, may God grant us the strength to do what we know must be done.
Pull back the curtains. Let truth unfold. Deal with it.
Remember it all comes down to love.
And love is truly what matters.

Wading in the Creek:
When have you made a sacrifice for someone?
How has someone sacrificed something for you?
Do you take others into consideration when you make decisions?
When have you avoided the truth?
Why do you fear confrontation?

Swimming the River:
Write a story with this line "…and there it was staring me in the face!"

Write a narrative of a time you were overly dramatic about a situation.

Write a dialogue between two brothers making a compromise over who gets to drive their father's car.

Write a poem about a charismatic character.

Write a man vs. nature scene.

On Regret

Concerning ourselves of the past is wasteful because we can't change it. We must place ourselves in the power of now.

The errors of your past are no place to dwell. There's no need to linger in the shadows.

Admit when you are wrong. Forgive yourself. Forgive others.

Accept what is right here and now. Simply put, move on.

Know no one is perfect, but learn from your mistakes.

Face it...you can't change the past. No use wasting time and energy trying to control what is already done.

Living each moment fully engaged will pave your future; this is where your power exists.

Be gentle with yourself. Be gentle with others.

Do the best you can each day. Create peace wherever you travel.

You are not who you were yesterday, nor are you who you will be tomorrow.

Focus on love and kindness. Deal from a place of gentleness.

When you refuse to live in yesterday or get lost in the future, you permit yourself to be present here in this moment; you allow yourself to walk the path unfolding before you.

Don't keep looking over your shoulder. Life waits before you.

Take in everything as you walk on your way. Don't take anything for granted.

Keep walking, one step at a time. Happy traveling.

Wading in the Creek:

What things from your past still control you?

How do actions of your past affect choices you make now?

How do you think having made different choices would have impacted your life?

What is the most important lesson you've learned from an action you've taken?
What process do you use to lead you to the choices you make now?

Swimming the River:
Write a short story about someone whose life has been guided by a regret of the past.
Write a free verse poem using the following words: choice, star, regret, power, and dungeon.
Write a scene of showing someone riddled with regret. Don't use dialogue. Show guilt through actions and mannerisms.
Write a persuasive piece about the power of forgiveness.
Write a personal narrative/ memoir about a difficult choice.

Living with Grace and Gratitude

Live your life in a way which reflects gratitude for your blessings.

Sometimes we take life for granted.
We forget how blessed we are. We think about what we don't have or wish for things we don't necessarily need rather than enjoy what we have here right now. While all parts of the rose are essential, we tend to focus on two parts, the thorns and the blossom. We scorn the thorns for the pain they cause and delight in the beauty and the fragrance of the blossom.

We treat life in the same manner. We reject the aspects which discomfort or embarrass us and take pride in those we feel are worthy.

Sometimes we don't even see the beauty of the petals because we are too focused on the thorns. Those are the times we have to strip away what distorts our view so we may see the beauty of our lives.

As beautiful as the flower of life is, it is so because of its thorns, leaves, stem, and all the parts that make the flower bloom. Our lives work the same way. Every aspect of our lives to this point in time has shaped us into who we are today.

Appreciate life. Be grateful for your blessings. Know you are important to others.

Thank God for your life. Thank your family and friends for love.

Live and love with grace. Choose to be happy.

Wading in the Creek:
For what things in life are you most grateful?
Which experiences do you feel have had the greatest influence on creating who you are today?
How do you feel the blossoms of your life outweigh the thorns?
Do you use your thorns in a healthy manner?
What do you offer to others that you do not expect in return?

Swimming the River:
Write about the aspects of your life as body parts. Which parts lead what areas?
Write a personal narrative/memoir about something negative turning into a blessing.
Write a dialogue between sisters. Have one be an optimist and the other a pessimist.

Write a haiku about thorns.
Use nature as a setting to create a mood of peace or discontent.

Secret Rooms of Our Lives

We are houses of many rooms, all of which need upkeep.

We each have secret rooms within us. These are the rooms that hold our dreams and fears.

Sharing our fears makes us vulnerable. We allow access to only those we trust.

Voicing our dreams can make us feel like we're setting ourselves up for failure in the eyes of others if we never attain our goals.

We seek solitude to restore a balance others are unable to provide us. We need our private rooms to sort out our pain, contemplate life, and make choices.

The disruption of the uninvited unsettles us. This reminds us not to intrude the space of others.

It's permissible to knock on the door, but don't enter unless the room unless the homeowner welcomes your presence. Respect for boundaries is vital in relationships.

Visit your own secret room. Curl up and drift off in a dream. Rise and open the curtains to let the sunshine bounce against the walls. Dance across the floor. Feel the coolness of the hardwood floor beneath your bare feet. Sing and let your voice rise to the ceiling. Smell the wild honeysuckle as it winds its way along your path. Taste the salt of your tears and know what gives your life meaning.

Enjoy your room. Know it is yours, whether you wish to share it or not.

Wading in the Creek:

How do you share or hide your fears?

How best are you able to balance dreams and reality?

Which dreams are you most afraid to voice?

In what ways do others respect your boundaries?

What do you do in your private time to rejuvenate your spirit?

Swimming the River:

Write a couplet about your house.

Write a story about someone living in a secret room in a house.

Describe your secret inner room. Use this for a personal essay on soul searching.

Describe a favorite room in your house. Use this to write a short story from the room's point of view.

Write a scene where a neighbor is trying to invade another's personal and physical space.

It's All in How We Look at it

How we view the world indicates how we behave in it.

We usually see things the way we want to see them, not always as they are.

What we see depends on what we are looking for. We focus on what is important to us and lose the details.

We complain when things are not as they seem, yet we blow things out of proportion.

We make things brighter, bigger, and more important than they really are. We deny or avoid matters which need our attention.

When we concentrate on things that don't really matter in the big picture we miss the point. Learning to see things through a different perspective prevents us from distorting our vision.

Step out of the view and the picture changes.
Remove the lens of emotion and it shifts again. Don't be dominated by the familiarity of your subject.
It takes more than vision to see. When we access the tools we're gifted we are resulted with a panoramic view.
Take the time for a second look. Change your lens. Refocus. Zoom in or out. Do you still see what you saw the first time?

Wading in the Creek:
In what ways have you benefitted by changing your perspective?
When have you been wrong about how you looked at something or someone?
When have you avoided the truth by refusing to see what was in front of you?
What is the biggest mistake you have made by focusing on something that was not important?
How have you hurt someone or been hurt by circumstances blown out of proportion?

Swimming the River:
Write an essay concerning the difference of perspectives when looking from the outside in and looking from the inside out.
Write a poem about a fish eye view.
Write a scene playing out the steps of denial. Use a vivid setting to support the unfolding event.
Write a short story where someone is focused on a small unimportant detail.
Write a dialogue between people with differing viewpoints on a piece of art.

To Save Our Souls

Connection keeps our souls from rusting.

We appear polished and poised. We adorn ourselves in jewelry, makeup and fashionable clothing. We hide financial troubles and personal heartaches beneath a smile. We make ourselves presentable to the prying public. From the outside looking in, all is well in our world.

The stress of the façade gets heavy. Instead of admitting our shortcomings we stop showing up. We are embarrassed. We fear humiliation and abandonment. We shut our doors and disappear inside ourselves. We push away those who try to get in.

When we lock the doors on life we forget how to reach out. We even go as far as locking our souls to ourselves. We bury our dreams and lose our passions. We turn our backs on life.

We know we've gone too far, but we can't seem to stop ourselves. We don't know which road leads home, nor do we know if we can repair this home we've built around us. When we allow the dust in our lives to turn to oceans of sand we fear the waves. We prepare to be washed away. We settle beneath the dunes and the wild grasses grow upon us. We forget the purpose of water. We don't allow it to wash away the debris or use it to cleanse our souls.

Water can offer us a new beginning. Fill a bucket. Grab a sponge. We can start where we are. The inside of our homes portray our true structure. It is never too late to clean house. Never be afraid to ask someone to hold the dustpan while you sweep the broom.

Wading in the Creek:

What has driven you to build walls to keep people out?

When have you been too afraid to ask for help?

Have you ever been so focused on one aspect of your life you've let other parts go?

How have you or someone you know managed to return from a place of disrepair?

If things aren't as they appear in your world, why do you present them as such?

Swimming the River:

Write a personal narrative/memoir about the steps taken before a public appearance.

Write an essay about people not taking care of their own needs.
Write about a neighborhood helping clean up a (physical or literal) mess.
Write a scene about someone visiting a friend and finding her emotionally distraught and her house in disarray.
Write a poem about "the way things appear to be".

Bare Bones of Life

No matter how hard we try to hide, who we are deep within eventually rises to the surface.

What is this stuff that holds us together? I don't mean the composition of you and me as a pair. I mean the workings within each of us as individuals that run far deeper than fake smiles and waves of our hands. I'm

not talking about promises, handshakes, or whispers in the dark.
When all the pretty colors are stripped away and the bones of the matter are all that's left, who are you?
Are you a jumbled mass of confused principles? Or are you a backbone of sound morals?
When the dressing is removed, true character remains. Are you a conductor of truth?
A conveyor of wisdom? A person of good intention or appropriate means? Do you simply speak or do you deliver?
When you are disrobed of the scarlet and golden hues of life and the winds of time have worn you down, will you break and collapse to a heap on the ground? Or will you be strong enough to bend and sway but stand your ground?
May we each learn to shed the leaves of indifference and share the value of our experiences.
May we unite in goodness to move this world forward. May we learn there is power in love.
One day at a time, one step at a time, may we share our lives from the backbone.

Wading in the Creek:
Is your moral structure based on the way you were raised or constructed from life experience?
How is your public persona the same or different from your authentic self?
Which of your characteristics would make you want to be friends with yourself?
When have you been waved by principle?
When have you compromised but still held tight to your integrity?

Swimming the River:
Write a poem about bones.

Write a story based on someone trusting his/her body.
Write an essay about the origin of instincts. Are they located in the heart, head, or backbone?
Write a personal narrative/memoir about a physical appearance hiding a weakened inner structure.
Give the core of your being a name and write a character profile.

Reaching for Soul

If you want validity from others, cherish them for who they are. The benefit of true relationship is infinite.

From first look this bush appears kind of homely with its scraggly burnt crimson buds. When you step a bit closer, you are taken in by its spicy aroma.

Soon you are absolutely smitten.

The fragrance calls to you.

The blossoms twinkle in the sunlight.

Even the dying buds curl into tiny art formations.

You become enthralled with the season of the bush...early spring you look for the first buds.

You delight in the aroma as the wind shifts in your direction.

You watch the red buds dance until they crumble to the ground.

You mourn the completion of the season.

The season of the soul is much the same as the season of the bush.

Often we don't give those without stellar looks the chance to charm us.

And how often have we been disappointed to find the beautiful to be self-absorbed or mean spirited?

Sometimes we are pleasantly surprised to find those we like the most to be people we have passed by.

Maybe we thought they were unapproachable when really they were just shy.

How often have you felt misunderstood? Not valued? Do people give you the same attention as you pay others?

The next time you meet someone, look a little deeper. You never know what rests deeper than the eye can see.

Take the time to take a second look at those you see every day. There might be something you've been overlooking. Listen to the words they speak and the tone in which they say them. Observe their actions. Spirit deserves more than to be skimmed over. Give people a chance. Get to know them.

Ever received a fabulous gift wrapped in newspaper?
What a pleasant surprise it is!
We are just packaging, some fancy while others plain.
Our gifts are held inside.
Pull the paper back and experience the life that awaits discovery.
Everyone yearns to be known.

Wading in the Creek:
How do your actions match your words?
Do you take the time to know the people you are involved with?
Has there been a time you've been disappointed to know someone on a deeper level?
How do you feel valued by your friends and family?
In what ways do you feel you are wrapped in fancy or plain paper?

Swimming the River:
Write a story about a package left on a doorstep.
Write about seeing an object at a distance and how different it looks close up. Detail how it looks both near and from afar.
Write a personal narrative/memoir about reconnecting with someone from the good old days.
Write a scene of someone slowly opening a gift. Does the opener have stiff fingers? Is he/she savoring the moment or trying not to tear the paper? Is this person supposed to be opening the present?
Write a poem including the words dance, crumble, value, and discover.

Illumination

Each time we perform an act of kindness we light a candle. Together we can unite the world in light.

We often walk in darkness. Sometimes of our own choosing, other times not.

We see not the sun, moon, or the stars as they pierce clouds to brighten the sky.

We merely exist while life shines all around us. The shadows within us provoke fear and put us on edge.

A random act of kindness or the warmth of love in our lives can be enough to break through the barrier. We see the light in the moment, the wonder of our lives, and in the world beyond us.

When we are moved by compassion, we want to pass the torch. We can place our flames together and hold the world in love and light.

May each of our hearts touch one another and together we can illuminate the world in the beauty of love.

Wading in the Creek:
Do you ever feel like you are living your life in darkness?
Are you a morning or night person?
When do you feel "brightest"?
Are you compassionate?
Why do you think sunlight lifts most of our spirits?

Swimming the River:
Write about a time you got up much earlier than usual?
Write a story about a group of kids/teenagers staying up all night. Why are they up? What are they doing to stay awake?
Write a scene where an unfeeling person is moved by compassion.
Write a poem about wonder.
Write anything (fiction or nonfiction) including "It really seemed like a good idea…"

Must We Bend Because We Can

Love empowers our flexibility in ways nothing else can.

We claim to be flexible. We generally go with the flow. We try not to be judgmental. Our hearts are open. We love. We hurt. We forgive. We accept. Well, most of the time. And when we can't we beat ourselves up about it.

We consider ourselves to be trees when it comes to bending. We sometimes bend willingly and other times when forced. We're strong enough to bend fairly far and bounce back without snapping off. However, not all of us can twist and turn in the air...we are not contortionists. We still have roots. We are bound by those roots.

There are times in life we establish relationships purely for the sake of others. We take others in because we love the same people. We become products of the relationship. Those relationships might end due to miles of separation, divorce, or even death. The relationships might continue because we've grown to love and trust these newcomers in our lives.

We have the power to cut relationships off, let them wane on their own, or we can choose to nurture its continuance. There are times we feel we have bent as far as we can. Our hearts need to know if the other person is willing to bend.

Then there are times we feel betrayed when we find the friendship is based on falsehoods. We know connections based on a sea of deceit cannot swim nor even float. We realize it is a vast whirlpool waiting to drown all who venture too close. We slip into a grieving process of denial and anger, enough to make us refuse to bend anymore. Maybe we're stubborn. Maybe we're prideful. Maybe, our devotion sides with our roots. But maybe we need only set boundaries, and allow love to take care of the rest.

Wading in the Creek:
Do you consider yourself to be a fair person?
How do you balance the needs of others with your own?
Has there ever been a time you considered yourself a martyr?
If you have you severed relationships in your life, why?
Do you allow people to take advantage of you?

Swimming the River:
Write an essay explaining the difference between adjustment and sacrifice.
Write a scene in which someone snaps.

Write a poem about elastic without actually using the word.

Write a story about someone floating down a river on a raft.

Write a personal narrative/memoir about taking advantage.

It's a Beautiful World

Bask in the stillness so you might know the beauty of life.

It is a beautiful world. So walk in it.
Enjoy these gifts which have been bestowed upon us.

Let your senses take over and transport you away
from the worries of the world.
Get out and see what nature has to offer.
Inhale the pungency of pine and cedar or the
sweetness of wild honeysuckle.
Feel the cool tickle of early morning grass beneath
your bare feet.
Taste the salt of the sea air. Savor the fruits and
berries of the earth.
Bask in the warmth of a tangerine sunset.
Listen to the songs of flowing rivers and whistling
winds.
You can choose to be transported by the beauty
around you
and still be right here, right now.
Get out of your head and into the world.
Enjoy this day for all its worth.

Wading in the Creek:
Do you recycle?
In what ways do you respect nature?
Do you give thanks for this world in prayer?
Are you the type of person who notices the beauty of
nature?
To what natural element do you feel the strongest
connection?

Swimming the River:
Write a poem about the taste of the sea.
Write a story with the setting on a boat. Is this a
docked houseboat or a sailboat on the sea? Use your
environment to set the tone of your story.
Write a scene about flying kites.
Write a personal narrative/memoir about childhood.
Choose an outside setting and include all senses.

Observe the sunset. Write about what is happening where you are beneath the setting sun.

Keeping Life's Drama in Perspective

We have a choice in the role we play in drama. Don't just give a performance. Be pleased with the part you play.

Drama can easily take over our lives if we allow ourselves to be sucked in. When emotions are high, we lose focus. We function on adrenaline and emotions. We react differently while in the heat of the moment. If we can remove ourselves from the situation things often look differently. However, sometimes the damage is already done. Even when damages occur, our reactions can still determine the outcome. As difficult as it might be, sometimes no reaction at all can be best. And then again, I wonder if that is just a coward's way out by not wanting to get involved. Most of us always have an opinion, but for the sake of peace we might keep it to ourselves.

At any rate, most dramas vary somewhat but have many commonalities. Some plays are tragedies, others comedies and some are spectacles. Drama always has a star player. It usually has supporting actors and an audience. Maybe more than anything it needs a critic to close it down.

Drama often occurs when someone is not getting what he/she wants or feels slighted. It can also start from a misinterpretation of what someone has said or done or from miscommunication in general. We might be the ones spreading false information. We might be the one whose words or actions have been misinterpreted. Or we might merely be innocent bystanders. One can apologize, walk away, or participate. (Are you still on stage? Are you continuing to watch to see what happens? Did you leave the building?) Whatever reaction one chooses in his/her role determines the outcome of the drama. It can fold production or it can go for an encore.

In life we find dramas being carried out with different casts in our families, groups of friends, politics, churches, P.T.A.s, and organized sport teams. How do we keep from getting sucked in? I prefer to stay clear of drama as seldom anything good comes from it. However, we all get involved in one way or another at one time or another. Are we starring in the show, selling tickets, or watching the play? Must we stick around to see the ending? Is the theme of the drama pertinent to our lives?

I usually consider myself a spectator in life. I like to watch what is going on around me. I'd rather slip in and out than be cast in a starring role. I learn more this way, am able to keep my emotions in check, and am less stressed. Am I missing out? I don't think so. I play an active role in my own life process. I only prefer to stay out of the politics of everyday living that surround me. I think there's a difference between actually living life and living in the midst of drama and politics. Some choose to live loud and open while others choose a more subtle approach to life. We are all stars of own life dramas, and the world is our theater. How we want to be perceived and remembered is up to us.

Wading in the Creek:
Do you get caught up in needless drama?
Do you act before you think?
When has reacting gotten you in trouble?
What areas of your life involve the most theatrics?
How do you avoid family drama?

Swimming the River:
Write a poem (Terza Rima) about a final act.
Write a story about a family drama. Make it a tragedy.
Write a personal narrative focusing on an event in which you were the star player. Make it a comedy.
Write a dialogue between a husband and wife. Have the husband advise the wife not to get involved in something that is none of her business. (or vice versa)
Write a scene where someone is performing damage control in a touchy situation.

Coloring a Life

Live a life worthy of framing.

The outline of my life has been drawn.
I've had the freedom to pick and choose my colors.
It's up to me to color in the picture.
Only I can bring this sketch to life.
Do others see the possibilities within me?
Who dares to draw my future for me?
I refuse to connect someone else's dots. I will draw my own life.
Through time my outline has stretched to include all the eye does not see.
I am much more than an image, a sketch, a photograph.
I am a life. I exist in living color.
I am all that purple dares to be, yet I am a calming ocean blue.
I am scarlet, a sizzling fire, that melds to a yellowed moon.

I am the green grasses of home and the brown of forests deep.

I am all that hides beneath the darkness and all that sparkles within ice.

Maybe I should erase my outline and leave a rainbow instead…

After all, life is possibility.

As difficult as it is to read the inside story of a black and white photograph, it's impossible to read the colors of a black and white life.

I'm off to buy some color markers. Better yet, I think I'll make my own paint.

Wading in the Creek:

Are you living your life according to someone else's plan?

What relative are you most like?

What makes you tick?

Do you enjoy your job?

Do you tend to make life more difficult than has to be?

Swimming the River:

Find a black and white photograph of someone you've never met and write a colorful character sketch for this person.

Now write a story about this person doing the unthinkable in his/her time.

Write a poem titled "In Living Color".

Write a colorful scene/setting using descriptive words without using colors.

Write a dialogue between someone who sees life in black and white and someone who lives life in color.

Blossoms of Beauty in this Life

We never leave beauty behind. It travels in our smiles, with our behaviors, and deep within our hearts.

We often hear of the sweet fragrance of cherry blossoms. Cherry blossom fragrance is faint, not sweet, more of an earthy scent. Not overwhelming, it lightly grabs your attention as it wafts through the air. As you turn to find the origin of aroma, you are taken in by the physical beauty. These delicate pale pink petals, almost paper thin, reach out and pull you in with their gaze. They seem to be nothing more than eye candy to many. To the birds and the bees, they are sustenance, shelter, hope and possibility.

I look at these blossoms and think of how beauty and scent linger long after one has walked away. Have you ever known someone who has remained with you long after his/her departure? Have you ever known someone whose memory brings a smile to your face and fills your heart with warmth?

I carry people in my heart for a lifetime. Their kindness and humility often propel me to be a better person. The combination of their love and compassion is a beauty which far surpasses physical realms. I absorb them, and shall remember them fondly as long as my mental capacity will allow. While I might be attracted to people of physical beauty, it isn't enough to keep my attention. There has to be a genuine benevolence about them to win me over.

I for one, and am sure you as well, would rather be remembered for being real and down to earth rather than a sickly sweet kind of fakeness. I think each of us want to be remembered by the beauty of our actions.

May we each become a lovely scent or glimpse of beauty that brings a feeling of goodness to someone. Show the world your beautiful heart; love with all your might.

Wading in the Creek:

Do you love freely or must others earn your love?
Are you taken in more by beauty or action?
What stays with you longer, a person's physical appearance or the way they make you feel?
How do you think you will be remembered?
Have you ever met anyone who appeared beautiful to the world but was not nice once you got a personal glimpse?

Swimming the River:

Write an obituary citing only actions of the deceased rather than dates and names of those left behind. Be expressive rather than specific. Be sure to use all senses in your description.

Write a personal narrative/memoir about the deception of beauty.

Write a poem about humility.

Write a dialogue between one of your physical attributes and one of your inner ones.

Write a story about how a memory of someone stays with and guides a group of people.

When People Aren't Who We Think They Are

We may never figure out other people, but we do have the power and responsibility to know ourselves.

Sometimes people surprise us. They even outright shock us when they turn out not be who we thought they were. The clues might have been right in front of our noses the entire time. Perhaps we didn't want to see the truth. Maybe the truth is so deplorable we can't understand how we overlooked it. Maybe we just want to think the best of people we think we know because we care about them.

We are often shocked to hear of atrocities people commit on the news. We wonder how they sleep at night. We wonder if they thought they wouldn't get caught. We wonder if they carry remorse for their actions. We feel sorry for their families. We're glad we don't know them. What happens when it turns out to be someone you know? Is it possible to support a person without condoning his actions? How do you deal with what you consider betrayal? How do their actions reflect on your relationship?

There are people we believe to be kind and generous individuals. Sometimes they have problems we are not aware of. Unbeknownst to us, they might be addicted to alcohol, drugs, sex, or gambling. They hurt people in the process of supplying their own needs. They might not mean to hurt people, but everyone within their path is affected in some way. We are disappointed in them and ache for their families. We are disappointed in ourselves for having been deceived. Our pride hurts. We ache for what never really was.

So how well we really know others? We can be friends with people for years and not know them on an intimate level. We only get to know people as well as they allow us. You can work with someone for many years and still have no idea what they do when they leave the workplace each evening. You can go to church with someone and work charitable events with them and not have any idea what kind of a person they are inside. You assume because they go to church and give to charity they are good inside…and maybe they are but just got caught up in something bigger than them.

How well does the average person really know himself? Maybe he knows what he likes or dislikes. Does he really know what motivates him to make the decisions he does in life? Is it his genetic makeup? Is it his belief system? Is it his personality? Is it his environment? Is it his family? What propels him to move forward in life? Does he reflect on his choices to help him know himself and push him to become a better person?

The next time you are shocked at someone's action or reactions, think about how well you really know that person. Do you know him well enough to predict his movements? Is he really who you think he is or do you only know the mask he is wearing? Do you see something isn't quite right? Are you close enough to offer assistance? Are you who everyone thinks you are? Finally, do you even know who you are?

Wading in the Creek:

Is there a part of your past you hide from your friends?

Are there things your friends know about you that your family doesn't?

Do you wear a social mask?

Are you a different person at work?

Do you know what motivates your actions?

Swimming the River:

Write a story about a family who has found out one of their members has committed a crime.

Write a personal narrative/memoir about misrepresentation for the purpose of benefitting.

Write a poem about discovery.

Write a scene where someone is caught or found out. Be creative with your setting.

Write a detailed sketch of someone who lives a double life.

The Great Escape

Denial is as tenacious as a sandbur, but once we're free of it we feel so much better.

To a degree, denial is a coping mechanism. As long as we don't face whatever the ugly truth is, it doesn't exist in our minds. We deny truth because we don't know how to deal with it.

We often have an inkling that something is amiss, but avoidance seems easier than dealing with issues head on. If the consequences are life-altering, we'd rather stay within our comfort zone as long as we can. It might be a problem at work or home or a situation involving someone we love. We might not want to experience the pain or discomfort confrontation can bring. Most likely we are afraid of the changes that will happen in our lives. We tend to think life is simpler when we continue as we are. Waiting can make things worse as tension builds in the relationship and time accrues damages.

We want to stick to our own agendas, not what we think life is throwing at us. We're afraid of what others might think. We are not ready to see things for what they are. Maybe, we don't have faith that we will get through the consequences. When we deny truth we do not live in reality; we live in a fog, a haze.

Denial seems safe when we don't know how to cope with truth. We are overwhelmed with possibilities of what might happen. We alter, exaggerate, or disregard facts. We don't want our lives to be disturbed or disrupted from our normal routines. We feel threatened by confrontation. We are insecure for our futures. We repress our feelings. We act as if nothing is wrong, and it eats away at us.

We all snuggle up to and hold steadfastly to this thing called denial. There are times we don't want to face facts about other people, nor do we want to admit our own motives for choices we make. As difficult as it is to find someone close to us is not who we thought they were, it's even harder to acknowledge our own fallacies. We usually come out stronger after dealing with obstinate circumstances.

It is human nature to try to escape reality at times. The safety of denial is short lived. Generally, the longer we wait to confront truth, the more difficult the situation becomes. The upside is we usually prove to be more resilient than we give ourselves credit.

Wading in the Creek:

Do you deny problems or attack them head on?
What obvious circumstances have you refused to believe?
After facing the truth, how were you able to put your life back together?
How do you handle confrontation?
In what ways has a difficult situation changed your life?

Swimming the River:

Write a dialogue revealing a shocking truth.

Write a scene involving consequences of an action.

Write a poem about circumstance.

Write a story about a group of friends in denial about another friend's death. Is it their relationship to the victim or the circumstances behind his/her death that has them in denial?

Write a personal narrative/memoir about facing the truth.

Rocking the World

When we accept support in the same ways we give it, we will live in connection.

When we stand alone, it might be by choice, ours or others. It's possible that we stand alone on principle and don't follow the crowd. We might distance ourselves because we need time to be alone, to think things through, and to reflect on our lives. There are times we just don't want to be intruded upon. We might be tired or down on ourselves. We might just be shy and desire to be invited and accepted into the fold. We might have been alone so long we've started

growing moss on our souls. It takes a bit of dusting off
and courage to step back into those once familiar
surroundings or to seek a new place to call home.
We feel uncomfortable when we've been displaced.
We dislike being picked up and thrown into unfamiliar
territory where we don't fit in. We feel topsy-turvy and
out of sorts. We might be in the midst of attempting a
new challenge or we might be a bit different from
those that surround us. We long for the security of
home and the warmth of friendship. When we find the
right environment our beauty will shine through.
We want to be among friends where we are accepted.
We desire companionship. We want to know we are
loved and appreciated. We embrace relationships.
We don't always crave solitude. Sometimes we need
others to help us find our place in the world.
Sometimes we are the mountain range. We are stone
strong and sitting on top of the world. We provide a
place to rest. We nurture the life around us. We rise
towards the heavens and lift those within our reach.
Because we are the ones holding others up, we might
feel like nothing can knock us down. We will stop at
nothing to shelter those we love from danger. We're
strong enough to secure each mountain and gentle
enough to embrace the wind. We might find we can't
do it alone. We have to work together to keep the
storm at bay. We will roll, stack, and mold to form
walls to keep unwanted forces out and to keep the
fragile from slipping away. We will hold hands and
solidify our forces. There are times it takes more than
one to hold a family together. Teamwork
produces staggering results.
We become weathered by life and smoothed by time.
Living creates the lines and grooves that have form
and shape us. We're spread out, cupping and
angling at just the right places, and though we may be

cracking and chipping we're strong enough to remain steady. We like who we've become. We find peace within ourselves and others find comfort with us. Possibly the hardest and most seemingly unyielding places create the ones of greatest comfort and acquiescence.

Wading in the Creek:
How have you grown from hard times?
When have you sought shelter?
Have others looked to you for protection?
When have you felt hard or cold as stone?
When have you refused to help a family member?

Swimming the River:
Write a story about "moving mountains".
Write a scene of a community barricading their town from a storm.
Write a poem "solid as rock".
Write a personal narrative/memoir concerning an unyielding situation.
Write a dialogue between family members involving a sensitive family issue.

All Roads Eventually Lead Home

Having someone help us carry the load enables us to travel twice as far. Not to mention, it makes the trip more enjoyable.

Many paths are well worn. Many have treaded before us. We often prod on even though we have no idea where the path leads. Perhaps, the most extravagant of life's beauty awaits us at the end of the trail.
Now and then rocks or trees will block our paths. We must learn to climb, crawl, and scoot. Otherwise we must turn around. With each hurdle we leap, we are

empowered to take on a more rocky and winding road.

Some of us have treaded the grasses of our own pursuits so often we've formed our own road. Though we think we know exactly where we are going, surprises might be waiting just around the corner. Being courageous enough to continue opens new worlds for us to discover.

Trails often change; we lose our footing, or encounter the unexpected along the way. We might know where we're going but feel the need to be able to stop quickly, back track, or take another route. When there aren't any signs, instinct should be heeded. While the road we are traveling may seem long, the adventure and scenery along the way can make the journey worthwhile.

Some of us insist on traveling on solid ground. There are many crossings to keep us from getting our feet wet. When pitfalls can't be avoided, perhaps the tumble is an opportunity to learn a lesson. Bridges are frequently necessary to complete our passage.

The way might be well paved and close to home. The way might be small and comfortable. The ruts and bumps may be few and the ride smooth. Many of us travel the same route over and over simply because of its familiarity.

There are times we speed along. We might need to slow down and grab a rail on our journey. There is no shame in taking a rest or asking for a hand to guide us. There are times we need to be reminded to focus on the journey and not the destination. We decide we don't really want to be headed in that direction at all. There are many roads that lead to the same goal. Who is to say which the correct one to take is? Stepping on the grass between the stones won't make our journey any slower or alter the outcome; but it might cushion the movements making our trek more enjoyable. Buffers pad the falls.

When the road paved with good intentions abruptly ends, what do we do? Who says dead ends are really the end of the road? We can turn back, veer off, or we can trudge on fearlessly constructing the way for others to follow.

Wherever we travel we must do so with eyes and ears wide open as the weathers of life can put us in danger or lead us astray. We might have to voyage through storms to gain wisdom and experience which enable us to appreciate our purpose.

We are not meant to travel all roads. There will be times the way is specifically detailed for users, and we are not invited. Though we might not be able to travel that same route, we can always watch and learn from the experiences of others. Journeys are always best when the lessons are shared.

Sometimes, someone else is leading the way. The destination is clearly marked. The traffic is clear. We might be able to move ahead, pass others, and get there faster. But it really doesn't matter who gets there first if it's really where we belong. We don't always realize how significant the journey is until we reach our goal. We must learn to savor the journey because we will reach our destination before we know it. May it be said of us all we were wise and happy travelers.

Wading in the Creek:

Are you a weary traveler?
Do you stop to rest when you're tired?
Why do you travel alone or with others?
Are you learning lessons along the way?
Are you afraid to take the road less traveled?

Swimming the River:
Write a poem "detour".
Write a story about an alternate route.
Write a personal narrative/memoir about a dead end.
Write a dialogue between a traveler who wants to turn around and one who wants to trudge through difficult terrain.
Write a scene set at a crossroads.

Finding Middle Ground

Love and acceptance create the backbone of life's relationships.

Everything blends together for beauty and purpose. We hold one another up and we grow together in our experience. Together we are the recipes for excellence and success.

We assist others and we all prosper. We need one another. We can do more together than we can alone. We benefit from the comfort of the shade and the light of the sun. Our differences complement one another while our likeness keeps us in agreement.

We learn to compromise, adjust, and thrive. Satisfaction waits for those who seek it.

Sometimes we provide the peace, and other times we simply bask in its presence.

What we produce comes back to us. When we provide and accept support, the outcome is a peaceful scene.

Balance is the secret. Give the love. Feel the love. Harmony will work its way into your life.

Wading in the Creek:

Do you help others?

Do you allow others to help you?

Does it upset you when others are not of the same opinion as you?

Do you feel you blend in or stand out in your family or group of friends?

Why are you willing or unwilling to compromise with other people?

Swimming the River:

Write a short story about someone with a steadfast belief and thinks everyone else is wrong.

Write a personal narrative about the most difficult compromise you've ever made or someone made to accommodate you.

Depict a scene with a setting that depicts a tone of agreement.
Write a scene where an employee prospers at the expense of a coworker.
Write a poem about blending.

Like a Bird on a Wire

When we are hard on ourselves we hinder our efforts. When we treat ourselves with kindness we set ourselves on the route of success.

What you see depends on your position on the perch, your relationship to the situation. Looking through the slant of emotion you view life from a small frame. When your view is limited you tend to make assumptions.

Sometimes you see only what you want to see. You see what's important to you, what affects your world. Like a bird on a wire, from a distance you have a larger view of the scenario. When detachment opens the field, you begin to see players other than yourself. When the subject you're observing is yourself you can't simply look in the mirror for answers nor can you ask those around you. You must delve deep within to find answers which might be as confusing as the questions.

Step outside of yourself to know your capabilities. Look at yourself from a new perspective. Trust your own worth and ability.

What is it you want to do? What makes you feel complete? What is your gift? Whatever your answers might be, you CAN get there from here. Take the first step today.

Be the bird on a wire, confident in his footing, sure of his surroundings, and ready to soar. Know you are one of a kind…only you can do what you have been brought here to accomplish.

Know you are capable. Trust your instincts. Believe in yourself.

Wading in the Creek:

Do you feel it's time to rewrite your story?

What can you say to yourself for motivation?

Under what circumstances do you most trust your instincts?

When do you feel most capable?

Do you get more encouragement by believing in yourself or having others believe in you?

Swimming the River:
Write a scene of a parent encouraging a grown child to believe in him/herself or vice versa.

Write a personal narrative of a situation you now see differently than when it was happening.

Write a story with a bird as the main character. Tell what this bird sees and hears below; write his interpretations of life beneath his wings.

Write a dialogue between "courage" and a character. What might courage say to motivate this character?

Write a poem about capability.

I leave you with the same final words I left you with on **Stepping into the Wilderness**. These words hold the same importance to me now as they did then.

May Your Blessings be Abundant

I wish for you a life of simple abundance; an abundance of necessary tools to learn to bend with the wind, stand strong against the tide, and forge trails across life's arduous mountains.
I wish for you the gift of time, moments of explicit joy with those you love. I want you to open your hands wide and let time escape and settle in your heart. I wish for you time to touch the morning; to feel the cool wetness of dew as it clings to the grass beneath your feet. I wish for you the time to see birds in flight; to notice the perfection of each single feather giving lift and how they join a myriad of others to create a formation which soars the vast blue skies. I wish for you the stillness of time to hear that voice; the one that calls deep within and guides you among the living. I wish for you the opportunity of time to taste the salt of the ocean so that you may enjoy the sweet pungency of earth. I wish for you time to smell the fragrance of daily living; the bittersweet scent of disappointment so you may savor the aroma of fulfillment. I wish for you time to know the value of living.
I wish for you the gift of vision so you might see the colorful rainbow of your life; the possibility of who you can become and the immeasurable value of who you are.
I wish for you the ability to take sorrow and weave it into a basket of hope; that you might know strength is

developed through adversity, and character is built by conquering fear and overcoming obstacles.

I hope you will learn to accept defeat as a rung on the ladder of success. I wish you the wisdom to recognize success as you walk along its terrain and know the valleys and peaks are not measured upon the opinions of others.

I desire patience for you to wait your turn, to know your timing is not always yours to choose. I wish you to be able to let go of control and allow your life to flower of its own accord.

I wish for you prosperity; to know it does not always come in material form and the intuition to feel the richness laden within the layers of your soul.

I wish for you faith not only in times of distress; but to know you are always loved in every moment and in every situation.

I wish for you mercy upon your own mistakes and forgiveness toward others. I wish for you a grateful spirit; an appreciation of those around you and all you are offered in this life. I wish you grace to pave a life of love.

I wish for you a generous heart, compassionate soul, good intentions, and a life of positive influence.

I pray for many moments of happiness in your life, but more importantly joy because joy is not merely a feeling but a condition of existence. More than this I wish you peace, a comfort which resides deep within and transcends all understanding.

I wish you conservation of your own well-being: I pray for your good health that you will make wise choices and reap the benefits of walking in comfort to enjoy every step of your journey.

I ask that you know the difference between being alone and being lonely; that you will find comfort in yourself and strength in knowing you are never truly alone.

I wish for you trust in trying times and compassionate hands to reach out and pick you up when you are down.

I wish for you to know the importance of limitations but also the freedom and power to step outside of self-imposed boundaries.

I wish you the desire to let go of anger and shame and replace them with a calm spirit and self-worth. I wish you acceptance of your past as it has created your beautiful soul of today.

I wish you work to challenge your being, play to enjoy life's pleasures, and rest to recharge your faculties. I wish you the opportunity to teach your craft and to serve others and the poise to receive the same. I wish you balance among your many interests and harmony in your life.

I pray your struggles are few and far between and never more than you can bear. I also pray you grow from your experiences and your healing be fully restored.

I wish for you clarity in times of chaos and discernment in times of doubt; that you will continue to reach when you feel nothing within your grasp.

I pray you recognize the many gifts in life which are free to those who reach for them. I pray you will continue to dance among the wildflowers while you reach for the stars.

I pray you will not feel you are entitled to life but blessed to live it.

I pray you will view the power of surrender as an act of acceptance; that you will both give and receive daily as needed.

I wish you immeasurable love and continuous light in all you encompass.

Whether your needs are physical or spiritual I pray your thirst might be quenched and your hunger satisfied all the days of your life; that you know your visit here is not absolute but life and love ring eternal. May you find a piece of heaven in all you touch on earth.
May you may always live your life as poetry in motion.

~Susan Carter Payne

www.ingramcontent.com/pod-product-compliance
Lightning Source LLC
Chambersburg PA
CBHW070657290526
45790CB00001B/352